Diana Athill was born in 1917. She worked for the BBC throughout the Second World War and then helped André Deutsch establish the publishing company that bore his name. For almost fifty years she was widely regarded as one of the finest editors in London, as well as a considerable and unjustly neglected writer. Two of what she called her 'documentary' books, *After a Funeral* and *Instead of a Letter*, are also published by Granta Books as is her novel, *Don't Look at Me Like That*. She lives in London.

Praise for *Stet*

'Good books about publishing are as hard to find as good publishers. To write well about the profession requires candour, wisdom, clarity, passion, a sense of proportion and above all a sense of humour . . . fortunately, Diana Athill has them in abundance' Blake Morrison, *Independent on Sunday*

'She is part of a distinguished tradition of book editing' *Economist*

'An elegantly-written account of five decades dedicated to books and writers' P.D. James

'Athill has written a short book long on charm . . . She tells her own story lightly and delightfully' *Daily Mail*

'Looking back on our first meeting, it was vintage Diana: high intelligence, 100 per cent sincerity, pessimism about the prospects of literature in the marketplace, and great vagueness. Reading this memoir of her professional life is like having her in front of me. Some writers' authorial voices are quite unlike them; Diana's is a distillation of herself. She doesn't write well, she writes wonderfully well, rather better than most of her writers' Timothy Mo, *Spectator*

'The mark of creative people is that "they react to experience directly and each in his own way". Her account of her career demonstrates, both in the exact lucidity of the telling and in what is being told, that she is one of them' *Sunday Times*

'An affectionate chronicle of a vanished era of independent literary publishing, before the emergence of the conglomerates' *Irish Times*

'All hail, Granta! This imprint should be classified as national treasure for its act of cultural affirmation in publishing Diana Athill's *Stet*. For me, the book could have been twice, thrice, its length, whether about the trade or about authors' *Publishing News*

'A delicate , amused self portrait as well as a study of some great writers and their little ways. All would-be authors and editors should h~~...~~ : Chisholm, *Sunday Telegraph*

Don't Look at Me Like That
Instead of a Letter
After a Funeral
An Unavoidable Delay
Make Believe – A True Story

STET

an editor's life

Diana Athill

Granta Books
London

Granta Publications, 2/3 Hanover Yard, London N1 8BE

First published in Great Britain by Granta Books 2000
This edition published by Granta Books 2001

A CIP catalogue record for this book
is available from the British Library.

1 3 5 7 9 10 8 6 4 2

Typeset in Minion by M Rules
Printed and bound in Great Britain by Mackays of Chatham plc

With love to
Edward Field and Neil Derrick
dear friends and encouragers

PART ONE

1

SOME YEARS AGO Tom Powers, an American publisher who is also a writer and historian, kindly told me I ought to write a book about my fifty years in publishing. He added: 'Put in all the figures – that is what one wants to know.' With those well-intentioned words he nearly finished off this book before it was begun.

Partly – as I shall explain – from conditioning, and more – I am pretty sure – because of some kind of mental kink, I cannot remember figures. When I recall the various houses I have lived in in London I can see the colours of their front doors, the way the steps leading to those doors were worn, what kind of railings guarded their areas; but not one of their numbers can I remember. My bank account has had the same number for years and years, but I still have to consult my chequebook every time I need to produce it. When I needed to tell one of my authors how many copies of his or her book we were printing, I could – having all the material to hand – tell them; but ask me three months later, was it three thousand or five, and I would not know. The only publishing figures that remain with me are the shaming £25 we paid Jean Rhys for an option to see her novel *Wide Sargasso Sea*, and the impressive (at that time) £30,000 we were paid for the serial rights of Franz von Papen's memoirs.

But surely I could research the figures?

No, I could not.

Soon after André Deutsch Limited, the firm of which I had been one of the directors since it was founded almost forty years earlier, was sold to Tom Rosenthal in 1985, Tom sold its complete archive to Tulsa University in Oklahoma, and I have neither the money nor the energy to go to Tulsa and dive into that mountain of paper. And I confess that I am grateful for those lacks because of another one: good researchers enjoy researching, which I have never done, and I am not going to develop the instinct for it now that I am in my eighties. So I am sorry that this will not be the useful kind of book which would interest Tom Powers, but there it is.

Why am I going to write it? Not because I want to provide a history of British publishing in the second half of the twentieth century, but because I shall not be alive for much longer, and when I am gone all the experiences stored in my head will be gone too – they will be deleted with one swipe of the great eraser, and something in me squeaks 'Oh no – let at least some of it be rescued!'. It seems to be an instinctive twitch rather than a rational intention, but no less compelling for that. By a long-established printer's convention, a copy-editor wanting to rescue a deletion puts a row of dots under it and writes 'Stet' (let it stand) in the margin. This book is an attempt to 'Stet' some part of my experience in its original form (which happens to be sadly short of figures). Other people have given better accounts of our trade (notably Jeremy Lewis in *Kindred Spirits*, which is not only a delight, but also says everything which needs saying about what has happened to publishing, and why). All this book is, is the story of one old ex-editor who imagines that she will feel a little less dead if a few people read it.

The story began with my father telling me: 'You will have to earn your living.' He said it to me several times during my childhood (which began in 1917), and the way he said it implied that earning one's living was not quite natural. I do not remember resenting the idea, but it was slightly alarming. This was because my great-grandfather on my mother's side, a Yorkshire doctor of yeoman stock, had made or married the money to buy a beautiful house in Norfolk with a thousand acres of land, which seemed to the children of my generation to have been 'ours' from time immemorial. It was largely because of this place that my mother's family was the one to which I felt that I belonged. My father's had lost money, not made it, so they had no land for us to feel rooted in. They had taken off from Norfolk to Antigua in the seventeenth century, had done very well as sugar planters, but had eventually fizzled out financially with their trade, so that by my time several generations of Athill men had taken the earning of livings for granted. But even on their more down-to-earth side, mine was the first generation in which this applied to daughters as well as sons. Daughters would not, of course, have to earn their livings if they got married, but (this was never *said*) now that they would have to depend on love unaided by dowries, marriage could no longer be counted on with absolute confidence.

Not until recently, when in my old age I began to ponder my career in publishing, did it occur to me that my family background had done a lot to determine the nature of that career.

In 1952, after working with André Deutsch for five years in his first publishing firm, Allan Wingate, I became a founding director with him of his second firm, to which we gave his name. I can therefore say that for nearly fifty years I was a publisher, but the truth is that I was not, and it was my background that prevented it.

Although for all my life I have been much nearer poor than rich, I have inherited a symptom of richness: I have a strong propensity for idleness. Somewhere within me lurks an unregenerate creature which feels that money ought to fall from the sky, like rain. Should it fail to do so – too bad: like a farmer enduring drought one would get by somehow, or go under, which would be unpleasant but not so unpleasant as having blighted one's days by bothering about money. Naturally I always knew that one did in fact have to bother, and to some extent I did so, but only to the least possible extent. This meant that although I never went so far as to choose to do nothing, I did find it almost impossible to do anything I didn't want to do. Whether it was 'cannot' or 'will not' I don't know, but it felt like 'cannot'; and the things I could not do included many of the things a publisher had to do.

A publishing firm is a complicated business which has to buy, sell and manufacture or cause to be manufactured. What it buys and sells is products of people's imaginations, the materials for making books, and a variety of legal rights. What it manufactures is never the same from one item to the next. So a publisher must be able to understand and control a complex financial and technical structure; he must be a smart negotiator, good at bargaining; he must have a shrewd instinct for when to lash out and when to penny-pinch; he must be able efficiently to administer an office full of people, or to see that it is efficiently administered; and above all he must be able to sell his wares in all their forms. Against this, all I have ever been able to do with money is spend it; I loathe responsibility and telling people what to do; and above all I am incapable of selling anything to anyone. Not being a fool, I was well aware of the importance of all the aspects of my trade which I couldn't and didn't want to master, and even came to know a fair amount about them. But although I felt guilty about my own incapacities, the only part of the business that I could ever bring myself *truly to mind about* was the choosing and editing of books. This is certainly a very important part of the publishing process, but without all the rest of it, it would amount to nothing.

So I was not a publisher. I was an editor.

And even as an editor, a job which I thoroughly enjoyed, I betrayed my amateurish nature by drawing the line at working outside office hours. The working breakfast, and taking work home at weekends – two activities regarded by many as necessary evidence of commitment, both of them much indulged in by that born publisher, André Deutsch – were to me an abomination. Very rarely someone from my work moved over into my private life, but generally office and home were far apart, and home was much more important than office. And whereas I was ashamed of my limitations within the office, I was not ashamed of valuing my private life more highly than my work: that, to my mind, is what everyone ought to do.

In spite of this, being an editor did enlarge and extend my life in a way for which I am deeply grateful. It gave me a daily occupation which brought in enough money to live on and which was almost always enjoyable, and it constantly proved the truth of that ancient cliché about working in publishing: You Meet Such Interesting People. The first part of this book is about the daily occupation. The second part is about some of the people.

2

ALTHOUGH MY FAMILY contributed to my limitations in publishing, they prepared me well for editing. Asking myself what were the most important things in my childhood, I get the answer 'Falling in love, riding and reading'.

They all started early. I can't have been more than four when I first fell in love, because surely someone who attempted communication with the beloved by leaning out of a window and spitting on his head can't have been older than that? He was the gardener's 'boy', his name was Denis, he had melancholy brown eyes, and every day he manned a green iron hand-pump by the back door to provide us with bath water. Each crank of the pump-handle was followed by a splosh in the tank in the attic above the lavatory – rich, cascading sploshes to start with, gradually turning to meagre little sploshes. One day, hearing the pump at work, I went into the lavatory to lean out of the window and gaze fondly down on the flat cap below, until I became unable to resist the longing for communication, collected a mouthful of saliva, and spat. He felt it, looked up, those beautiful brown eyes met mine – and I shot out of the lavatory, scarlet and breathless with excitement. After which I was never, so far as I can remember, out of love.

The riding, too, started earlier than it could properly be done. When my mother, instead of Nanny, took me out she disliked pushing the pram, so a strange little saddle shaped like a miniature chair was strapped onto an aged pony and I was tied into it, to be led over grass instead of pushed along paths – a lovely improvement, heralding many years of being on a pony or a horse pretty well whenever I was out of doors.

And reading started with being read aloud to, which went on to overlap with one's own reading because my grandmother (we lived near her for many years) read aloud so beautifully that we never tired of listening to her. She might be doing a Beatrix Potter or the *Just So Stories* for the little ones, or *Uncle Remus* or *The Jungle Book* for the middle ones, or *Kim* or a Walter Scott (skipping the boring bits so cleverly that we never knew they were there) for the bigger ones, and whichever it was, everyone would be listening because she made them so marvellous. And everywhere we looked there were books. In our own house they were piled on tables and chairs, as well as on the shelves; and in Gran's house, where we so often were, they rose from floor to ceiling all round the library, along one whole wall in the morning-room, on three walls of my grandfather's study, along the full length of a passage called 'the corridor', and along three-quarters of a wall in the nursery. At Christmas and birthdays about eighty per cent of the presents we got were books, and no one was ever told not to read anything. My grandmother's father had been Master of University College, Oxford, and my grandfather, who wooed her when he was an undergraduate, had written several prize essays (which she kept and published privately after his death) which suggest by their distinction that he must have thought about becoming a professional historian before his father's death made him a contented landed gentleman. It never occurred to anyone in that family that reading could be a duty, so it never occurred to me. Reading was what one did indoors, as riding was what one did out of doors: an essential part of life, rather than a mere pleasure. As I grew older and 'You will have to earn your living' changed from being something my father said to being a real prospect, I was not bold enough to imagine myself worthy of work in publishing, but I would never have doubted that such work was the most desirable of all.

If publishing was too glamorous for me, what was I going to do? I was reasonably intelligent, I had been to Oxford ... but I had certainly not qualified myself for anything while there. Indeed, it was at Oxford that my idleness found its fullest expression and all I did there was having the best time of my life. Teaching was, I supposed, a possibility, or nursing; but both inspired in me the sensation of being faced with a bucket of cold porridge. And I didn't really know of any other kind of work. A vast difference between then and now is that then a middle-class Englishwoman in her early twenties could, without being exceptional, know not a single woman of her own age who was in a job. I had a fair number of friends, but to none of them could I turn for guidance.

Before the problem could become truly agitating it was blown away by the beginning of the Second World War, which made it unnecessary – even impossible – to think in terms of a career. You had to bundle into whatever war-work offered itself and get on with it. If you liked it, lucky you. If not, that was just a part of the general bloodiness of war and you expected yourself to endure it without making a fuss.

I was lucky. After a couple of false starts I was given a nudge towards the BBC by an Oxford friend who happened to have found a job in its recruitment office and thought I would have a chance of getting into a new information service that was to be attached to Overseas News. I did get in, and was allowed to stay there until the end of the war. I forget which Ministry it was that controlled the matter, but all jobs were reviewed from time to time, and if you were seen to be making no contribution to the war effort you were directed into something more useful. Telling the Overseas News Room who General de Gaulle was or how much oil was produced by the wells of Ploeşti was work classified as essential, so my wartime lot was an easy job shared with pleasant companions. The job was easy because an information service is only a matter of knowing where to look things up – and anyway, in those days the BBC confused *The Times* with Holy Writ: you showed someone a cutting from *The Times* and he believed it*.

---

* The BBC's Information Services were initiated by a man called Bachelor, who had built up the same kind of service for *The Times*. We used to laugh at our customers' dependence on the newspaper, but the truth was that thanks to Mr Bachelor it was amazingly well-served with information. It had a slight edge on us because its press-cuttings library had been going for longer and was therefore larger; but we were no less admirably structured and no less keenly scrupulous. By the time I got there Batch, as we called him, had become too grand to be often seen by his minions, but he was undoubtedly brilliant at his job.

3

W ITH ONE OF those BBC companions, after a while, I launched into flat-sharing. Until then I had lived in billets while our office was evacuated to Evesham in Worcestershire for safety's sake, and in a sequence of depressing bed-sitters when we were brought back to London to await Hitler's secret weapons, the flying bombs and the long-range missiles. The flat was the two top floors of a stately house in Devonshire Place, one of the streets traditionally inhabited by England's most expensive doctors who had left a temporary vacuum in the neighbourhood when carried away by the war. Marjorie and I had the top floor, which included the kitchen. George Weidenfeld and Henry Swanzy had the floor below us.

The few young men in the BBC at that time had to be exempt from military service. George was exempt because he was still an Austrian, Henry because . . . and I suddenly see that I don't know why Henry was exempt, which speaks well for the Second World War compared with the First. In the First a feverish jingoism prevailed, with women thrusting white feathers on men simply because they were not in uniform. In the Second I never saw or heard of any jingoism. Perhaps Henry was disqualified for active service by some weakness in his health, or perhaps he was a conscientious objector who was considered more useful in the BBC than down a coal-mine. Probably I once knew, but if so it was unimportant to me and my friends. Anyway, there he was, sharing the flat at first with George and a man called Lester Something, and when Lester moved away from London, with George, Marjorie and me. George was wooing Marjorie at the time, so our inclusion was probably his idea.

The men's floor had an enviable bathroom, all black glass and chrome, given extra distinction by containing a piano on which Henry often played moody music. Our bathroom was very mere – it had probably been the maids' – but the kitchen gave us an advantage since what communal living went on in the flat had necessarily to centre on it. Neither Marjorie's parents nor mine questioned the propriety of our ménage – but whether this was because they chose to believe us unshakeably chaste, or because we avoided mentioning George and Henry, I no longer remember.

The two of us who ended up in bed together were Marjorie and George. She fell seriously in love with him, causing some of our colleagues to exclaim 'Yuck!' and 'How could she?', because George at twenty-four already had a portly presence and a frog face. But he also had five times the intelligence of most of the young men we knew, and a great deal of sexual magnetism. I soon noticed – though Marjorie did not – that the women whose 'Yucks!' were the most emphatic were usually in bed with him before a month was out.

To be more exact, I did not notice this, but heard it from George himself, because in his early salad days he relished his sexual success too much to be discreet about it. He kept a list of his conquests at the back of his pocket diary, and would bring it out to show me when we were in the kitchen together without Marjorie. I remember him saying gleefully: 'Look – the fiftieth!'

At that time I was all but unsexed by sadness, because the man I was engaged to, who was serving in the Middle East, had first gone silent on me, then married someone else, then been killed. A little later I would start to find that promiscuity cheered me up, but our Devonshire Place days were too early for that. My inner life was bleak, which made surface entertainment all the more important. If Marjorie had been sailing into happiness with George I might have found the spectacle intolerably painful; but as it was, although I liked her and was far from wishing her ill, I found watching the relationship so interesting that it became enjoyable – the first time that I was shocked by my own beady eye.

After eight or nine months Lester came back and claimed his half of the apartment, so Marjorie went to live with her parents for a while and I returned to bed-sitters. Just before we left, our kitchen witnessed a significant event: the four of us chose a name for the periodical which George would soon be editing. After much list-making and many disappointments when good names turned out to have been used already, *Contact* was picked. During one of our naming sessions, when we had drifted onto other subjects and one of us asked George what his central ambition was, he replied: 'Very simple – to be a success.' So that was where George's publishing career began, and where its direction first became apparent; and soon afterwards, because of someone I met through George, my own publishing career put out the first pale tip of an underground shoot, like a deeply buried bulb.

*

Before this happened I had begun to feel a good deal better, partly because I had the luck to fall into a frivolous and enjoyable affair, and partly because Marjorie's mother's dentist told her that he wanted to let the top floor of his house in Queen Anne Street, which is a few minutes from Devonshire Place, and Marjorie and I took it. The dentist had converted this floor into an elegant little flat for his son, who had killed himself in its kitchen by putting his head in the gas oven – which we did not at first enjoy using. But soon we began to think that the poor young man must have had a weak personality, because no flat could have had a pleasanter atmosphere. Devonshire Place had been fun, but also uncomfortable and shabby to the point of squalor. Queen Anne Street was a delight to come home to.

So we decided to celebrate it by giving a party. George came, of course, and brought André Deutsch, the man who had introduced him to the publishing firm which was going to produce and distribute *Contact*: a firm which would soon cease to exist, called Nicholson and Watson. André, a Hungarian the same age as I was (twenty-six), had come to England to study economics, had been caught by the war, and had been interned as an enemy alien on the Isle of Man. The Hungarians were soon let out on condition that they reported regularly to the authorities, and André returned to London armed with a letter from a fellow-internee to a well-known bookseller who had passed him on to John Roberts, managing director of Nicholson and Watson. Roberts, a kind, lazy, rather boozy man who was struggling to keep the firm going almost single-handed, took him on as a salesman and was pleased to discover that he had acquired an intelligent and energetic young man who was greedy to learn every aspect of the trade: who was, in fact, finding his vocation. By the time André came to our party he was doing much more for the firm than visiting booksellers and librarians – not that I was bothered about that. He could have been a junior packer for all I cared. His being the first person I had ever met who was 'in publishing' was enough to exalt him in my eyes.

He was small, trim and good-looking in a boyish way. I remember thinking that his mouth was as fresh and soft-looking as a child's, and being surprised that I found it attractive – usually I liked my men on the rugged side. He sat on the floor and sang 'The foggy foggy dew', which was unexpected in a Hungarian, and charming, so that I was more aware of him than of anyone else in the room. Two days later, when he asked me to dinner and a theatre, I was gratified. He was living in a tiny house in a Knightsbridge mews, and that was impressive, too. The possibility of having a house had never entered my head. André's had been lent him by a friend who was away on war-work, but it seemed like his, which made him more 'grown-up' than I was. In that little house, after the theatre, we ate an omelette and went to bed together, without – as I remember it – much excitement on either side.

In old age I can still remember the matchless intoxication of falling in love (which may well be a neurotic condition, but still nothing else lights up the whole of one's being in that way) and the more common but no less delicious sensations of a powerful physical attraction; but I have gone blurry about the kind of affair I had with André. I wonder what took me into such affairs, and what held me in them, almost always, until the man moved on. Rather than remembering, I have to work it out.

It was not thinking myself in love when I was not – I was too clear-sighted for that. And it was not simply the nesting instinct, because I was romantic enough (or perhaps realist enough?) to be sure that I couldn't marry a man I didn't love. To start with it was probably curiosity – a cat-like impulse to poke my nose round the next corner – combined with the emptiness of my emotional life at the time: this would at least seem to fill it. And once it had got going . . . well, perhaps the nesting instinct did start to come into it, after all. Although I knew from experience that whenever I genuinely fell in love it happened almost on sight, perhaps in this other kind of affair I allowed myself to slide into a vague hope that this time, given the chance, love might develop. And anyway I was pleased to be wanted; I liked the social and erotic occupations involved; I enjoyed being fond of someone; and I continued to be moved by curiosity. Quite early in my career the image of a glass-bottomed boat came to me as an apt one for sex; a love-making relationship with a man offered chances to peer at what went on under his surface. Once, listening to someone as he told me for the third time a story about his childhood, I caught myself thinking 'He's a squeezed orange' . . . oh dear, the beady eye again!

It was soon apparent that André and I would not be lovers for long. I felt that I could have enjoyed making love with him if he had been more enthusiastic about making love with me, and given my essential coldness since the shock of losing the man I really wanted, he probably felt the same about me: less than adequate grounds for an affair. And he was an insomniac whose bed, though a double one, was not wide. When I wanted to sleep, he wanted to sit up and read *The Times*, and what he wanted to do he did, with much uninhibited rustling: it was his house, his bed – and insomnia commands respect while somnolence is boring. Englishwomen are notorious for somnolence, he told me tetchily. He often remarked on the shortcomings of the English as lovers, a habit shared by many continental men with a touching failure to see how easily it

can provoke the bitten-back response 'Who are you to talk?'. Rather
than enjoying the dozen or so nights we spent together, we went
through them 'because they were there', and the only sadness I felt
when he moved on to another bedfellow was the knee-jerk reaction
'There you are, you see – you're unable to keep *anyone*'.
Understanding that I owed this droopy feeling to the fiancé who
had jilted me, I didn't hold it against André. It turned out that the
slightness of our affair did not matter because – mystifyingly given
how unlike we are in temperament – we had ended it as friends.

We continued to meet, I became his confidante about his love-
life, and he introduced me to his other friends: a handful of other
Hungarians and three or four likeable and intelligent older women
who had more or less adopted him. Two of the women ran an
organization which helped to settle refugees, in which he had done
part-time work before being interned; one – Sheila Dunn, who
became a dear friend of mine – was the aunt of a girl he'd had an
affair with; and one – Audrey Harvey – was an old friend of Sheila's.
Because of my inwardly broken-spirited state, when we met I knew
no one in London apart from the people I worked with; while my
pre-war friends were scattered and out of reach. Even the merry
lover who had done me (and was still intermittently doing me) so
much good came from a neighbouring department of the BBC's
Overseas Service; and anyway we saw each other only to dine and
hop into bed because he was both married and busy. The sudden
acquisition of a group shading from slight but amusing acquaintances to great friends was an important pleasure.

The first flying bomb came over while I was lying awake in
André's bed. Its engine-sound was strange but we assumed that it
was a plane, and that the sudden silence followed by an explosion
as it landed meant that it had been shot down. The news next day

that it was Hitler's 'secret weapon', which we had all been trying not to believe in, was the most frightening news that had yet hit us. As well as fearing the pilotless engine-driven bomb in itself, you feared the idea of being panicked by it; so it seemed best not to think about it, and that was how most people dealt with it, confining their fear to the short time between first hearing one of the horrible things approaching, and feeling guilty relief when it chuntered past without its engine cutting out, to fall on someone else. When the V2s took over – huge missiles launched at us from hundreds of miles away – I thought them less bad because they came down bang, without a whisper of warning, so you might be killed but you didn't have time to feel afraid. (In retrospect I find them the more frightening of the two.) To get a good night's sleep, André and I sometimes spent weekends with Audrey Harvey, who lived about an hour by train from Marylebone Station. Sheila would be there too, and usually one or two of the Hungarians: how dear generous Audrey found suppers and breakfasts for us in those tightly rationed days I can't remember: I suppose we took our rations with us. These were delightful occasions, which contributed a good deal to the feeling of being 'family' which grew up between André and me.

It was this feeling which made it natural for us both to expect me to be involved in his plans when he decided that he would start a publishing house as soon as the war ended . . . not that my own expectations, to begin with, were anything but provisional. He had no money and no connections: how could he possibly start a publishing house? It was like someone saying 'When I win the football pools'. But of course if he *did* win them, I would want to be in on it.

He asked me one day – we were walking arm in arm down Frith Street – 'What's the minimum you'd need to earn, to start with?' I didn't know what to say. I would like it to be more than the £380 a year I was getting from the BBC, but I didn't want to sound greedy. Impatient with my hesitation he said: 'What about £500?' and I replied: 'That would be lovely.' It sounded a lot to me, but we were only talking about a dream so what did it matter?

We spent VE Day (Victory in Europe) together, milling about the West End in a mass of people who mostly seemed deeply relieved rather than over the top with joy. Certainly my own feeling, which I had to keep stoking up to overcome incredulity, was 'It's over!' rather than 'We've won!'. VJ Day (Victory over Japan) worked better – unlike more sensitive people among my friends I felt on that day no shadow of horror at the Atom Bomb: that came later. We were swept into the crowd which surged up the Mall to call the royal family out onto the balcony over and over again, and there was no resisting the mood engendered by that crowd. It was one of a joy so benign that it was no surprise to read in a newspaper report next morning that although people had stood all over the flower beds in front of the palace, they had placed their feet so carefully that hardly a single plant had been damaged.

4

ANDRÉ STARTED HIS first publishing house, Allan Wingate, late in 1945. I missed its first month or so because I did not leave the BBC until after July that year, then took a refreshing break at home in Norfolk. I know I was still in the BBC in July because a wonderfully exhilarating experience – more so, even, than VJ Day – was spending the whole night in the Overseas News Room when the results of the first post-war election were coming over the ticker-tape machine, and we gradually realized that Labour was winning. That *was* a matter of 'We've won!'. Other people's memories of the years just after the war often stress the continuation of rationing and 'austerity', and a sense of fatigue, but it didn't feel like that to me. Recovery was slow – how could it be anything else? – but it was going on all the time. Why fret when it was evident that things were getting better and better, and that society was going to be juster and more generous than it had ever been before? And for many years to come the existence, and smooth functioning, of the National Health Service was *by itself*

(how can people forget this?) enough to justify this now naive-seeming optimism.

One of the things I missed was the naming of André's firm. Before I left for Norfolk we had spent an evening together looking through the London telephone directory for a name beginning with D that he could feel at home with. (His father had written from Hungary, urging him not to use his own name, on the grounds that English people would think he was German and would resent him.) His reason for wanting to keep his initials was that he had just had them embroidered on some new shirts, the logic of which was as obscure to me then as it is now, and proved too flimsy to overcome his lack of response to any of the D-names in the book. Although I disagreed with his father (what about Heinemann?), I liked the name he hit on while I was away. It sounded so convincing that people sometimes said they were glad to see the firm in business again, as though we were reviving a house that had existed before the war.

By the time I got back to London André had rented an office – the ground floor of a late Georgian house in Great Cumberland Place, near Marble Arch – and had moved into it with Mr Kaufmann who was to be our accountant; two secretaries; Mr Brown our packer; and Audrey Harvey who had put up some of the capital and was to edit *Junior*, a magazine for children, under our imprint. Sheila Dunn, who drew well and wittily and made her small living as a commercial artist, was to come in part-time as Audrey's art editor, and a gravely handsome man called Vincent Stuart was to design our books on a free-lance basis. A figure in the background who remained shadowy to me was Alex Lederer, a manufacturer of handbags who had provided the greater part of the capital. My innate amateurishness is demonstrated by my lack of interest in how André persuaded this agreeable but alien being to cough up: it never occurred to me to ask. I did know, however, that our capital as a whole amounted to £3,000, and that it was generally held that no publishing company could make a go of it with less than £15,000: we were constantly reminded of that by André, as he urged us to recycle used envelopes, switch off lights behind us, and generally exercise the strictest economy in every possible way.

We had at our disposal a large front room, once the house's dining-room, with two tall windows and a pompous marble chimneypiece; a smaller back room – perhaps once the owner's study? – looking out into a well; a wide passage along the side of the well accommodating Mr Brown and his packing-bench; and at the end of the passage a lavatory and a small one-storey extension in which Mr Kaufmann lurked, which looked back across the well to the 'study'.

Although at the BBC I had shared an office with several other people, I was dismayed by the front room when I first saw it. André had his desk at one of the windows, Audrey hers at the other end of the room, and against the wall opposite the fireplace there was a rather handsome dining-room table almost hidden under piles of manuscripts, paper samples, reference books and so on – we had as yet no shelves, cupboards or filing cabinets. A corner of this table was to be mine, and Sheila was to use another corner on the two or three days a week when she would be in. It seemed likely that the work would need more concentration than anything I had done before, and here I would be, sandwiched in the exiguous space between the intense working lives of other people, with their animated telephone conversations and frequent visitors ... would I be able to endure it?

The discomfort I went through to begin with – there must have been some – has faded from my mind, but I remember clearly a moment which occurred after three or four weeks. It was lunch-time; I pushed aside my work and looked round the room. There was André arguing for better terms with a printer's representative, Audrey talking to one of her authors who had two children in tow, Sheila going through a portfolio of drawings with an artist. 'How amazingly adaptable people are,' I thought. 'Until I happened to look round this room, I might have been alone in it.'

My job was to read, edit, copy-edit, proof-read, and also to look after the advertising, which meant copy-writing and designing as well as booking space after André had told me which books he wanted advertised in which newspapers, and had given me a budget. Although reading and editing were by far the most inter-esting of my tasks, they did not at first seem the most important. This was because I could do them easily: I had read a lot and I was developing confidence in my own judgement. Against which I had never before even speculated as to how advertisements got into newspapers, and as soon as I had learnt what the process was I saw that I would be no good at an important part of it. Booking space was no problem, but after that was done I had to persuade the advertising manager of the paper concerned that although our space was a small one (usually a six or eight inch single column) it should be given the kind of conspicuous position usually occu-pied by much larger ads. This, to André's incredulous indignation, I hardly ever achieved, and almost every time I failed he would telephone the newspaper's man and tell him that next time he must give us an even better position to make up for his disgraceful fail-ure this time – which the wretched man would usually do. But not without imploring me to keep André off his back because he couldn't go on inviting trouble for himself by granting such favours. I was soon feeling sick at the mere sound of the word 'advertising', and the fact that I continued to carry this albatross round my neck for several years is evidence of the power André could exercise by the simple means of being utterly convinced that what he wanted was *right*.

Over the advertising he was aided by my own guilt at evading so many other disagreeable things: it was ample expiation. But his power *was* extraordinary. Watching him use it I often thought I was witnessing the secret of the successful pathological liar: the one who persuades businessmen and politicians to back crackpot ventures. The liar is, of course, helped by the greed and gullibility of his victims, but he could not succeed on a grand scale without the 'magical' persuasiveness which comes from utter self-persuasion. How lucky, I used to think, that André is by nature an honest man, or where would we all be?

Another of his characteristics which I learnt at this time was less useful – indeed, it was to be his great weakness as a manager of people. He saw everything not done *exactly* as he himself would have done it as being done wrong – enragingly wrong – and anything that was done right as not worth comment. Things often were done wrong to begin with, and his vigilance taught us a lot, but the apparent indifference which took the place of carping when all was well was discouraging. Sheila and I often pointed out that praise and kindness made people work better as well as feel happier, and he would promise to mend his ways, but he never did.

For a while my experience of this in connection with the advertising was painful. I think I was brave in the way I plunged into the unfamiliar task, and showed fortitude in overcoming my nature and going on with it for years in spite of loathing it (except for the bits which involved messing about with pencil, ruler and eraser, which I quite liked).

True to form, André was always sharply critical, not only of my feebleness with the papers' advertising managers, but also of the wording and spacing within each ad. For some time this was helpful, then the implication that I was bad at this boring task into which he had shoved me began to get at me, so though I could soon see for myself that my ads didn't look too bad, a muted drone of guilt was gradually induced, to underlie this side of my work.

It threatened for a time to underlie everything, because once André's nagging focused on someone it did so with increasing intensity. I was sometimes slapdash about detail which struck me as unimportant. I might, for example, forget (not when dealing with a book's text, but perhaps when typing out an ad or the blurb for a jacket) that it was our house style to use single quotation marks, reserving double ones for quotations within quotations. When something like this happened André's shock would be extreme. 'How can I go to Paris next week if I can't trust you over something as simple as this? Don't you realize what it would cost to correct that if it got through to proof stage?' . . . and there would be a slight crescendo in guilt's drone. And a creepy result was that one began to make more and worse mistakes. I was to see this happening over and over again to other people after the nagging had swivelled away from me (I came to envisage it as a wicked little searchlight always seeking out a victim). It could escalate with mystifying speed until you began to dread going into the office. You knew that justice was really on your side in that he was making an absurd and sometimes cruel fuss over small matters, but you had been manoeuvred into a position where you couldn't *claim* this without appearing to be indifferent to the ideals of perfection to which we were all devoted. I can still recall the sensation of tattered nerves which came from the mixture of indignation and guilt which ensued.

To polish off this disagreeable subject, I must skip forward a few months to a time when he returned from one of those trips to Paris (they were book-hunting trips) and asked me for the key of his car. 'What do you mean? I haven't got it' – and he exploded. 'Oh my God – you're impossible! I gave it to you just before I left. What have you done with it?' I was stunned: how, in six short days, could I have forgotten something so important? I struggled to recall taking the key from him and was unable to summon up the least shadow of it, but his conviction was absolute and my own aware-ness of my shortcomings was inflamed: I had to believe that he had given me that key, and I truly feared that I might be losing my mind. I went home in misery, worried all night over this sudden softening of my brain, and next morning it was all I could do to crawl back to the office.

André's car was parked outside it, and he was at his desk looking cheerful. How, I asked tremulously, had he got it started? 'Oh that . . .' he said. 'I didn't leave the key with you after all, I left it with the man at the garage.'

That silenced the guilt drone for ever, and soon afterwards I learnt to disregard unnecessary fusses when what he was com-plaining of was something being done in way B instead of way A, and how to forestall his rage when I had genuinely erred. It was simple: a quick resort to *mea culpa*. 'Oh André – I've done such a dreadful thing. They've spelt Stephens with a v on the back flap of the jacket and I didn't notice!' – 'Is it too late to correct?' – 'Yes, that's what's so *frightful*.' – 'Oh well, worse things have happened.

You'll have to apologize to Stephens – and *do* remember to get someone to give your jacket proofs a second reading.' End of scene. Once I had twigged that confession always took the wind out of his sails I had no more trouble from the 'searchlight'. But there would rarely be a time during the next fifty years when it was not making life a misery for someone, and working first in Allan Wingate, then in André Deutsch, would have been a great deal more pleasant if this had not been so.

One feels the lack of counterpoint when using words. Anyone reading the above account of André's nagging might wonder why I continued to work for him; but that was only one thread in many. I was doing and enjoying other parts of the job in addition to the advertising, while as for André . . .

It was not easy to summarize his activities. He read books; he hunted books; he thought books up; for several years he did all the selling of books, and the buying and selling of book rights; he bought paper; he dealt with printers, binders and blockmakers; he made all the decisions about the promotion of our books; he checked every detail of their design; he checked copy-writing, proof-reading, important letters; he soothed and cajoled the bank; he persuaded suppliers to give us unprecedented credit; he raised capital out of the blue when we could no longer pay our bills; he delivered books in Aggie, his Baby Austin named after its AGY registration number (I did that, too); if we were sending out leaflets he sat on the floor stuffing them into envelopes until after midnight and always did more to the minute than anyone else; and his own pulse was no more part of him than his awareness of our turnover and overheads. He also did all the firm's remembering – the car-key incident was unique. Usually his memory for detail was so good as to be almost frightening. He had learnt his way about his trade so rapidly and so thoroughly, and had committed himself to it so whole-heartedly, that it is not fanciful to describe him as someone who had discovered his vocation. One never doubted that the firm, having been created by him, was now being kept going by him: if he had withdrawn from it, it would have ceased to exist.

Dictatorships work: that is why they are so readily accepted, and if they are demonstrably more or less just, as they can be to start with, they are accepted with a gratitude more personal than can be inspired by other kinds of regime. In its miniature way André's dictatorship was strong for the following reasons: he had already learnt so much about publishing while those working for him still knew nothing; it was his nature to turn ideas into action without delay, which is a rare gift; while he paid us mingy salaries he also paid himself a mingy salary, and the company was so small that we could all see with our own eyes that there was no money available for anything else; when he was mean, chiselling down payments, scrounging discounts, running after us to switch off lights and so on, even though he was certainly not offending against his nature, yet he was still always and evidently doing it for the company's sake; and when he nagged and raged, even when it was maddeningly out of proportion with the offence, that too was always and evidently for the company's sake. Reasonable explanation of errors and amiable encouragement to avoid them would have been more effective as well as pleasanter, but if such behaviour didn't come naturally to him, too bad: we would have to put up with him as he was which, on the whole, we were glad to do. Sheila and I, in particular, who were the people closest to him, had such a habit of fondness for him that it never occurred to us to do anything else.

So there we were, the strain and gloom of war gradually fading away behind us, starting on a delightful adventure supported and exhilarated by the energies and abilities of the man who had launched it. Even if the ride had its bumpy moments there was no question of wishing to climb down.

5

I REMEMBER ALLAN WINGATE's first premises rather than its first books simply because the first books were so feeble that I blush for them. The firm kicked off with a list of four: *Route to Potsdam*, a piece of political journalism commenting on the Allies' plans for Europe, by Bela Ivanyi, one of André's Hungarian friends, the argument of which had no perceptible effect on anyone; *Beds*, a boring history of mankind's sleeping habits by Reginald Reynolds, to whom André had been introduced by George Orwell; *Fats and Figures*, a little book on diet, sensible but hardly more than a pamphlet, by a prison governor who was to become Lord Taylor; and the fourth has vanished from my mind. To start with André simply snatched at any homeless manuscript that happened to float by, and the reading public just after the war was so starved of books and so short of alternative forms of entertainment that almost anything (in our case almost nothing) could be presented by a publisher without looking silly.

A sad irony underlay this situation. While André was with

Nicolson and Watson George Orwell submitted *Animal Farm* to
them and John Roberts asked André to read it for him. André
declared it wonderful, but Roberts, when he heard what it was
about, said: 'Nonsense, laddie – no one nowadays wants to make
fun of Uncle Joe.' André, who was determined to help the penniless
and modest Orwell whom he saw as almost saint-like, decided that
Jonathan Cape was the right publisher for him, and Orwell took his
advice. Cape accepted the book, but shared Roberts's doubts to the
extent of making a condition: it must be checked by some sort of
official authority to make sure that it was not considered damaging
to the war effort. And it was so considered: His Majesty's
Government sincerely hoped that Mr Cape would refrain from
publishing something so sharply critical of our Soviet Ally – and
Mr Cape did refrain.

Orwell, who by this time was getting pretty desperate and who
knew that André was planning to start his own firm as soon as he
could raise a little capital, then said to André: 'Look, why don't *you*
do it? Why don't you start off your firm with it?' And André,
strongly tempted to pounce but still far from sure that he would be
able to start a firm however much he wanted to, felt that he must
not let a man he liked and respected so deeply take such a risk. No,
he said. And the essential resilience of his nature was later to be well
illustrated by the fact that the more famous *Animal Farm* became,
the prouder he was of his own early recognition of it and of his not
letting Orwell take the risk of giving it to him, with never a moan
at having lost this prize.

The first book we took on because of me still sits on my shelves,
and fills me with astonishment. André, through Hungarian friends
in Paris, had come to know several people in the French literary
world, among them Gerard Hopkins. Hopkins suggested that he

should look at the work of a writer called Noël Devaulx, so André brought back from a visit to Paris *The Tailor's Cake*, a tiny volume of seven stories which he dumped on my corner of the table: he couldn't read French while I, though I had spent no time with French people so had no confidence in speaking it, had been taught it very well and could read it nearly as easily as English. So the decision was to be mine.

There was a solemn awareness of responsibility. There was bafflement for a while, then an increasing fascination. These were surreal stories in which characters who assumed you knew more about them than you did moved through strange places, such as a busy sea-port which was nowhere near the sea, or a village in which everyone was old and silent except for foolish laughter, and which vanished the morning after the traveller had been benighted in it. Everything in these stories was described with a meticulous sobriety and precision, which gave them the concentrated reality of dreams. Perhaps they were allegories – but of what? The only thing I felt sure of was that the author was utterly convinced by them – he couldn't have written them in any other way.

I would soon begin to find such fantasies a waste of time – of my time, anyway – but then, in addition to liking the sobriety and precision of the style, I felt the pull of mystification: 'I can't understand this – probably, being beyond me, it is very special.' This common response to not seeing the point of something has a rather touching humility, but that doesn't save it – or so I now believe – from being a betrayal of intelligence which has allowed a good deal of junk to masquerade as art. Whether that matters much is another question: throughout my publishing life I thought it did, so I am glad to say that the publication of *The Tailor's Cake* in 1946, beautifully translated by Betty Askwith, was the only occasion on which I succumbed to the charm of mystification.

A more amusing aspect of that publication is that even in those book-hungry days we would have had to go far to find a piece of fiction more obviously unsaleable than those stories, yet once I had pronounced them good we didn't think twice about publishing them. And they cannot have been a hideous flop: given my sense of responsibility for them, and André's tendency to attribute blame, I would surely remember if they had been. It is sad to think that we did not appreciate the luxury of not having to ask ourselves 'Is it commercially viable?' in those happy days before that question set in.

At Wingate I was André's employee, not his partner. My opinion of a book might or might not influence his decision, but if he took something on without asking my opinion I accepted without question that it was my job to work on it whether I liked it or not. Usually my attitude was 'No doubt he knows best'. Partly this was a hangover from my original feeling that working with books was something for people cleverer and more serious than I was; partly it was a realistic assessment of my own inexperience; and partly – something which shocks me now that I recognize it – it was that old inherited idleness: it didn't really matter enough to me what he brought in, provided a large enough proportion of our books struck me as good enough.

The first of these to appear on our list were of a sober – almost stately – kind, a result of the post-war book famine which meant that the reissue of classics was felt as a need. Villon and Heine, for example. André had met a man called Bill Stirling who considered himself capable of translating all the major poets of Europe.

Although in this he was aiming too high, he did produce translations of those two which were up to appearing in good-looking bilingual volumes with which we could justly be pleased. We also produced a good edition of the novels and poems of the Brontë sisters edited by Phyllis Bentley, whose introduction stands up well against modern Brontë scholarship, and who included examples of their important juvenilia – the first time that had been done in a British edition.

Our first two money-spinners could hardly have been less like the above, or each other. The first was *How to be an Alien* by George Mikes. André had been at school in Budapest with George's younger brother, when he had glimpsed George enviously as a dashing grown-up. Meeting again in London, as exiles, they found that the years between them had concertinaed, and became friends. George's little squib on being a foreigner in England had an extraordinary success. Its foreign rights seemed to sell themselves, it is still in print today, and it was the foundation stone of a career as a humorous writer that kept George going comfortably until his death in 1990. It also brought in Nicolas Bentley, who would become our partner when André Deutsch Limited was founded. A book so short needed to be given a little more bulk by illustrations, and an author so foreign and unknown could do with a familiar British name beside his own on the title-page. André persuaded Nick with some difficulty to do twelve drawings for *Alien* – and was never to let him forget that he had been dubious enough about an alliance with these two flighty central Europeans to fight for an outright fee of £100 rather than a cut of the royalties. When André refused to give way over this, Nick almost backed out. I don't know exactly what he eventually made out of those twelve drawings, but it was certainly well over £10,000. Nick and his wife

Barbara were soon close friends of André and the woman who
became André's great love soon after he had launched Wingate, to
whom he would remain loyal for the rest of his life.

Our second money-spinner was *The Reader's Digest Omnibus*:
the first important chunk of loot brought home by André from
New York. He had seen at once how important an annual shopping
trip to the United States would be, and built up a network of good
relationships there with amazing speed. Knowing that he would
have trouble persuading Audrey and me that he was not disgracing
us all for life by taking on this project, he made no attempt to do so
but simply announced the *fait accompli* and told us we must lump
it. We did indeed wince and moan – I more than Audrey, because I
had to proof-read the thing and write its blurb. The Reader's Digest
may have changed by now – I have never looked at it again since
that intensive experience of it – but at the end of the forties its central message could fairly be represented by the following little story.
A man is faced with the choice between doing something rather
dishonest and making a fortune, or refusing to do something rather
dishonest and staying poor. Virtuously, he chooses to stay poor –
whereupon an unexpected turn of events connected with this
choice makes him a *much bigger fortune* than he would have gained
by the dishonest act. Looking back, I think that having started off
so prune-faced about it, the least I should have done for dignity's
sake was keep up the disapproval; but in fact the book's success was
so great, and so many people seemed to think that we had been
clever to get hold of it, that I ended by feeling quite pleased with it.

Two other books from those distant days were important to my
apprenticeship. One was a serious technical account of develop-
ments in modern architecture which revealed an incidental
pleasure to be found in editing: the way it can teach you a lot about

a subject unfamiliar to you, which you might not otherwise have approached. The other was about the discovery of Tahiti, which taught me once and for all the true nature of my job.

The latter book was by a man who could not write. He had clumsily and laboriously put a great many words on paper because he happened to be obsessed by his subject. No one but a hungry young publisher building a list would have waded through his type-script, but having done so I realized that he knew everything it was possible to know about a significant and extraordinary event, and that his book would be a thoroughly respectable addition to our list if only it could be made readable.

André had recently met an urbane and cultivated old man who had just retired from governing a British outpost in the Pacific, and who had said that he hoped to find the occasional literary task with which to fill his time. We brought the two men together, the author agreed to pay Sir Whatsit a reasonable fee for editing his book, and the latter carried it off, sat on it for three months, then returned it to its author with his bill which the poor man paid at once before forwarding his 'finished' book to us. To my dismay I found that lazy old Sir Whatsit had become bored after about six pages, and from then on had done almost nothing: the book was still unreadable. Either we had to return it to its author with a cheque to cover the expense we had let him in for, or I would have to edit it myself. We were short of non-fiction. I did it myself.

I doubt if there was a sentence – certainly there was not a para-graph – that I did not alter and often have to retype, sending it chapter by chapter to the author for his approval which – although he was naturally grouchy – he always gave. I enjoyed the work. It was like removing layers of crumpled brown paper from an awk-wardly shaped parcel, and revealing the attractive present which it contained (a good deal more satisfying than the minor tinkering involved when editing a competent writer). Soon after the book's publication it was reviewed in *The Times Literary Supplement*: an excellent book, said the reviewer, scholarly and full of fascinating detail, and beautifully written into the bargain. The author promptly sent me a clipping of this review, pinned to a short note. 'How nice of him,' I thought, 'he's going to say thank you!' What he said in fact was: 'You will observe the comment about the writing which confirms what I have thought all along, that none of that fuss about it was necessary.' When I had stopped laughing I accepted the message: an editor must never expect thanks (sometimes they come, but they must always be seen as a bonus). We must always remember that we are only midwives – if we want praise for progeny we must give birth to our own.

The most important book in the history of Allan Wingate was Norman Mailer's first novel, *The Naked and the Dead*, which came to us from an agent desperate because six of London's leading publishers had rejected it in spite of its crossing the Atlantic on a wave of excitement (it was one of those books, always American at that time, which are mysteriously preceded by a certainty that they will cause a stir). Our list had gained substance and our sales organization was seen to be good, but we were still too small to be any agent's first choice for a big book – or indeed even their seventh choice, had they not concluded that none of the more firmly established houses was going to make an offer.

The book was a war novel, all its characters soldiers going through hell in the Pacific, where Mailer himself had served. He was bent on conveying the nature of these soldiers and their experiences accurately, so naturally he wanted the men in his novel to speak like the men he had known, which meant using the words 'fuck' and 'fucking', and using them often. His American publishers had told him that although they knew it to be a great book, they could not publish it, and nor would anyone else (which appeared to be true) with those words spelt out. I believe the use of 'f—' was suggested; but 'fuck' and 'fucking' occurred so often that this would have made the dialogue look like fish-net, so 'fug' and 'fugging' were agreed as substitutes.

It might be argued that the six English publishers who rejected the book because of the obscenity of its language were less ridiculous than the American publisher who accepted this solution. Given the premiss from which they were all working, that 'fuck' was unprintably obscene, how could another word which sounded so nearly the same, and which was loaded with the same meaning, not be equally obscene? There has never, I think, been a clearer demonstration of the idiocy of making words taboo.

We, of course, pounced. It is many years since I reread the book and much of it is now hazy in my mind, but I still have a strong memory of a passage in which exhausted men are struggling to manhandle a gun out of deep mud, which makes me think that I was right in feeling that it was very good – a book which had genuinely expanded the range of my imagination. We wanted to restore the 'fucks' but dared not; and as it turned out we were right not to dare.

Review copies went out to the press about three weeks before publication, and the literary editor of *The Sunday Times* left his lying about in his office. The newspaper's editor, who was an old man nearing retirement, ambled in and chanced to pick it up and open it. The first thing to meet his eye was 'fug' ... followed by 'fug' and 'fug' again. So that Sunday, on the paper's front page, there appeared a short but furious protest, written by the editor himself, against the projected publication of a book so vile that (and he truly did use these words) 'no decent man could leave it where his women or children might happen to see it'.

As always on a Sunday I was sleeping late, so I was cross when I had to answer the front-door bell at eight-thirty. There stood André, unshaven, a pair of trousers and a macintosh pulled on over his pyjamas, and a copy of *The Sunday Times* in his hand.

'Read this!'

'Oh my God!'

I was as alarmed as he was. The book was printed and bound – the first printing was large – it was a long book, expensive to manu-facture . . . close to the wind as the firm was still having to sail, if this book was banned we would go down.

'Hurry and get some clothes on,' said André. 'We must rush a copy to Desmond MacCarthy – I've got his address.'

MacCarthy was the most influential reviewer then writing. We scribbled a note begging him to read the book at once and to say publicly that it was not obscene, then we set off in Aggie to push it through his letter-box. To insist on seeing him so early on a Sunday morning might, we felt, put him off. In retrospect, the chief value of our outing was that it was something to *do* in this nerve-racking situation: I don't think that MacCarthy's eventual response can have been more than civil, or I would not have forgotten it.

Next morning orders started pouring into the office, and only then did it occur to us that if we were not heading for disaster, it might be a triumph. Meanwhile we were instantly served with an injunction against publishing *The Naked and the Dead* until the Attorney General, Sir Hartley Shawcross, had considered the case and had given us permission to do so (if he did). Whether the injunction was handed over by the large and apparently amiable police detective who spent the morning questioning us all, or whether it came separately, I do not know.

During the next two or three weeks the flood of orders nearly submerged us, the frustration of not being able to supply them became acute, and the encouragement we received from everyone we knew began to make triumph seem more likely than disaster. Finally André persuaded an MP of his acquaintance to ask a question in the House of Commons about the book's fate: was the Attorney General going to ban it or not? The answer was no – a rather grudging one in that Shawcross said that he thought it was a bad book, but still no. So we were off – into, ironically, quite worrying financial problems, because we were hard put to it to pay for the several reprints we had to order.

What we gained from this adventure was more than a good and best-selling novel; more, even, than the presence of Norman Mailer on our list from then on. Overnight we began to be seen as a brave and dashing little firm, worth serious attention from agents handling interesting new writers, and André's welcome when he visited New York became even more richly rewarding.

6

ALLAN WINGATE'S PERFORMANCE looked quite impressive from the outside. Our books soon became more interesting and we produced them well – even elegantly – within the limits imposed by continuing paper rationing. (The quality of paper was poor, and there were regulations controlling the use of white space in a layout and so on, which made good typography a challenge for several years after the war.) And we were good, by the cottage-industry standards of the day, at selling. André's work as a rep for Nicolson and Watson had taught him a lot about booksellers and librarians (the latter our chief customers for fiction), and he never under-estimated the importance of good relations with them: again and again we were told how rare and pleasing it was for the head of a publishing house to visit and listen to booksellers, as he often did, and to be ready to negotiate directly with them about, for example, returning copies if they had over-ordered, instead of leaving such matters to a rep. To begin with he did this because we *had* no reps – no sales department, for that matter – but it was an attitude which stayed with him for all his career. He would always be liked by the people to whom we sold our wares – vital to a firm like ours, which remained short of books which the trade *had* to stock such as works of reference, how-to-do-its, and the cosier and flashier sorts of entertainment book.

From the inside, however, we looked wobbly. This was because the experienced people who said it was impossible to start a publishing firm on £3,000 were right. We were always running out of money.

Not being able to pay our bills used to give me horrible sensations of hollowness mixed with nausea, and I think that poor Mr Kaufmann, the man who actually had to do the desperate juggling which was supposed to stave off disaster, felt much the same. To André, on the other hand, these crises appeared to be invigorating, chiefly because he didn't feel 'I have run up bills I can't pay', but 'These idiotic printers and binders are trying to prevent me from publishing truly essential books which the world needs and which will end by making enough money to pay them all and to spare'. So although he recognized that he would have to raise some more money somehow, he was never debilitated. Instead he was inspired. Never, at the time when a crisis struck, did we know anyone who wanted to invest in a struggling new publishing house; but always, in a matter of days, André found such a person. My own way of weathering a panic was by thrusting it aside and concentrating grimly on what was under my nose – reading a manuscript, designing an advertisement or whatever – so instead of following his manoeuvres with the intelligent interest which would have made this account so much more valuable, I kept my eyes tight shut; and when I next opened them, there would be André, cock-a-hoop, with a new director in tow. This happened five times.

There was, however, an inconvenient, though endearing, weak spot in André's otherwise impressive life-saving equipment. He had come to England because he loved the idea of it. In the Budapest of his schooldays the language you studied, in addition to Latin, was either German or English, and he, influenced by a beloved and admired uncle, had chosen English without a moment's hesitation, and had found it greatly to his taste. The books he read as a result must have been an odd selection, because they left him with a romantic picture of a country remarkable for honesty and reliability, largely inhabited by comic but rather attractive beings known as English Gentlemen. I am sure that if, when he was trawling for someone to invest money in his firm, his net had caught a fellow-Hungarian, he would have insisted on their agreeing a thoroughly businesslike contract; but each time what came up was an Englishman – an Englishman radiant with the glow which shines from the answer to a prayer, and coloured a becoming pink by his viewer's preconceptions. So – it is still hard to believe, but it is true – what existed between André and these five timely miracles was, in each case, nothing but a Gentleman's Agreement. You couldn't even say that it wasn't worth the paper it was written on, because there wasn't any paper.

Before this process began we lost Audrey, because André was unable to tolerate her husband Ronald. Her investment had been made largely to provide Ron with a job to come home to when he was demobilized from the Army, and within a few months of our opening he joined us as sales manager. He was a gentle, serene-looking person, a listener rather than a talker, and what his previous occupation had been I never knew. After he left us he trained as an osteopath, at which he was successful. There was nothing about him of the businessman – and certainly not of the salesman.

Because none of us had met him earlier, Ron was not strictly an example of André's inability to see what people were like. This weakness related to his impatient and clumsy handling of staff, both of them stemming from an absolute failure to be interested in any viewpoint but his own. It was quickly to become apparent that if he wanted a particular kind of person for his firm – a fireball of a sales manager, for example, or a scrupulously careful copy-editor – then he would see the next man or woman who approached him as that person, and would impatiently dismiss any dissenting opinion. Before he was done he would cram innu-merable square pegs into round holes, and it is exhausting to remember the emotional wear and tear involved when, to his furi-ous indignation (against the poor pegs) he began to see them for what they were and they had to be wrenched or eased out. But in Ron's case it was bad luck rather than bad judgement – bad luck, especially, for Ron, who was not with us three weeks before he was pinned helplessly in the eye of that alarming little searchlight, was seen to be doing nothing right, and as a consequence began doing more and more things wrong.

Sheila and I, who both loved Audrey and liked Ron, tried to make a stand, arguing and persuading as best we could, but in vain. I remember when Ron's sin was paying a bill on demand, as I would have done in his place. 'That blockhead! Doesn't he know what credit means?' – 'But you can't yell at a man like that – have you ever *explained* to him that their bills don't have to be paid for thirty days? Why should he know that? He's never done this sort of thing before.' – '*I* didn't have to have it explained to *me.*'

Ron *was* the wrong person for the job, but by the time he and

Audrey decided that there was nothing for it but to pick up their money and go, what we would have to put up with for the sake of what we liked and admired in André had become uncomfortably evident.

Then the five timely miracles began, and brought us together again. They were all so astonishingly useless that it was impossible not to gang up against them. (Though none of them was quite so bad as one that got away because – by God's grace – he approached me not André. He was a charmingly camp old friend of my childhood who had married a very rich woman and wrote out of the blue to say that if we had a niche for him he would gladly put a lot of money into the firm. André quivered like a pointer, but it was I who was asked to lunch so it was I to whom my old friend said: 'Well, my dear, the chief object of this exercise is to give me something to do before lunch instead of getting drunk.' I often wondered how André would have managed to blank that sentence out if he had been sitting in my chair.)

Of the five, numbers one, two and three soon became discouraged, whereupon numbers four and five bought them out, thus ending up owning more of the firm than André did – and he with no scrap of paper to give him any rights at all. Neither of them was a crook; both of them to start with were ready to admit that André had created Wingate and that he was the person who put most into running it. With a lot of tolerance and tact it might have been possible for them and him to rub along together, but tolerance and tact were not at André's command.

Number four I shall call Bertie, because he looked and sounded exactly like P. G. Wodehouse's Bertie Wooster would have looked and sounded had he been in his forties. He was the son of a well-known middle-brow man of letters and had himself written several novels in which expensive sports cars figured more prominently than any human character (André used to say that the only thing that had ever given Bertie an erection was a Lagonda). He lacked business sense and common sense – indeed a nonsense was what he usually made of any of our daily tasks unless someone was breathing down his neck. I would take things away and quietly do them again, which naturally riled him, while André would attack him in an appallingly humiliating way.

Number five, whom I shall call Roger, had worked in publishing for years, but in an old-fashioned firm specializing in books on architecture and the British countryside, which had not demanded the expenditure of much energy. He knew the language of the trade, which was something, but he did not care to put himself out, and was often drunk (after, rather than before lunch, unlike my old friend). Occasionally he came in with a black eye, having been roughed up by an ill-chosen boyfriend, and he spent many of his afternoons in tears. (Roger was to end by killing himself – but at that time, on an acquaintance that was very superficial, I saw him only as foolish without understanding that he was also sad.) Perhaps he had thought he would work gently, between hangovers, on elegant books about eighteenth-century chinoiserie or Strawberry-Hill Gothick, but he never got round to signing up any such work and made no contribution to what we had on the stocks; so Roger, too, received short shrift from André. And, like Bertie, the more he was treated as an incompetent booby, the more he remembered that the two of them, not André, were now in financial control of Allan Wingate.

For a year or two this disastrous set-up bubbled and seethed, at first without the intervention of any outsider, then in the offices of lawyers. We had moved to more commodious offices near Harrods,

and now had a sales department and a production department
(but still no one in charge of publicity except me with my hateful
ads). In spite of our problems we were producing about fifty books
a year, most of them profitable, and we would have been exuber-
antly happy if we could have enjoyed Bertie's and Roger's money
without their presence. It seemed impossible, with everything
going so well, that André would be ousted from his own firm by
these two fools . . . but the more expert advice he took, the clearer
it became that this would happen. He hadn't a legal leg to stand on
and the best his lawyer could do was to wangle a 'generous' gesture
out of Bertie and Roger which allowed him, when he finally left, to
take a few cookery books and three or four very unimportant
others (he and I had agreed, once we had brought ourselves to face
the facts, that there was nothing for it but to start another publishing house).

There was, however, one book due to be delivered quite soon,
about which a decision was still to be reached. This was the memoirs of Franz von Papen. To quote my own catalogue description of
it:

Franz von Papen's life has faithfully reflected the fortunes of
his country for over half a century. As a boy, when he was a
court page in the Kaiser's entourage, he witnessed the
traditional pomp of imperialism. In his seventies, though
cleared of war guilt by the Nuremberg Tribunal, he
experienced defeat to the full when his own countrymen
sentenced him to imprisonment. Between these extremes he
was always at the centre of affairs in Germany, and whether
the balance he maintained was the result of a clear or an
ambivalent conscience is still a matter of conjecture.

His own interpretation of his career and the events with
which it was so closely connected is of the greatest
importance. He describes his activities as military attaché in
the United States from 1913 to 1915; he gives an account of
Allenby's campaign in the Middle East, as seen from 'the
other side'; he analyses the decline of the Weimar Republic,
which he knew both as a member of the Reichstag and as
Reich Chancellor. On the subject of his collaboration with
Hitler as Vice-Chancellor, his mission to Austria before the
Anschluss, and his appointment as Ambassador in Ankara
during the last war he is exhaustive. He does not shirk the
central enigma of his career: his acceptance of further high
office under the Nazis after his open criticism of their
methods in his Marburg speech, the murder of his
colleagues during the Roehm Putsch, and his own house
arrest.

This book is of outstanding interest, both as a
commentary on recent history from the German viewpoint,
and as a personal record.

To which I would add, now, that no one who hadn't just lived
through the Second World War can imagine how fascinating it
was, so soon after it, to hear one of *them* speaking.

This book the old man had been persuaded to write by André,
who had visited him in connection with *Operation Cicero*, the story
of the valet to the British Ambassador in Ankara, who towards the
end of the war had cheekily supplied the Germans with copies of
the contents of the ambassadorial safe. Von Papen, having been
our man's opposite number at the time, was in a position to confirm 'Cicero's' story (which at first sight seemed too good to be

true), which he did. André might, of course, have written to him about it, but characteristically saw greater possibilities in a meeting. Capturing the Cicero story was already one of his more striking achievements, involving a lightning dash to Ankara, but the way he used that book as a lead into another and more important project was an even better example of his energy.

Technically the memoirs he had secured would, when completed, belong to Allan Wingate, but even the lawyers felt that André had a moral right to them; something which Bertie and Roger were reluctant to acknowledge. The wrangling was bitter, but they did finally accept a suggestion made by the lawyers on the Friday which was André's and my last day at Allan Wingate: that there should be a 'moratorium' on the subject of von Papen until the following Tuesday, during which everyone should calm down in preparation for a decisive meeting about it.

On the intervening Sunday I went to André's house at lunchtime, to discuss our next move. While I was there the telephone rang, and hearing André switch to talking German it dawned on me that von Papen was on the line. Who, he asked, was this person who had just called him to say that André had been sacked from Allan Wingate? How could he have been sacked? What on earth was happening?

André, always quick on his feet, was never quicker than at that moment. The call had come as a complete surprise, the situation he had to get across was not a simple one, and he was trembling with rage at this sudden revelation of Bertie and Roger's sneaky manoeuvre; nevertheless in little more than ten minutes he had explained what was up with perfect lucidity and in exactly the right tone, and by the time he hung up he had von Papen's assurance that in no circumstances would Allan Wingate ever set eyes on his manuscript, which would be André's just as soon as he had launched his new firm. Seeing that silly pair of English Gentlemen being hoisted so neatly by their own petard remains one of the choicest satisfactions of my career.

This event also provided a solid foundation for André's new firm, of which I was to become a director. Within a very short time he had sold the serial rights of von Papen's book to a Sunday paper called the *People* for the sum (peanuts now, but awe-inspiring then) of £30,000.

7

1952: TWO THINGS ABOUT the new firm were certain from the start: it would be called André Deutsch, and André would be its absolute boss. There would be other shareholders – eight of them including Nicolas Bentley and me, who would be working directors – but the value of each holder's shares would be limited so that even if one of them bought out all the others, he would not gain control. A loan, soon to be repaid, enabled André to ensure this satisfactory state of affairs, and the von Papen serial deal lifted the firm at once into profitability.

My own investment, the minimum necessary to qualify me for a directorship, was £350 given me by my godmother. Like Nick, I was in it for the job. The other shareholders were in it as a friendly gesture to André, not as a business venture, although all would end by making a modest but respectable profit. It was a sensible and pleasant arrangement, and a profound relief after Allan Wingate – which, gratifyingly, died a natural death about five years after André's departure.

From the five Wingate years we brought friends on both the manufacturing and retailing sides of the book trade, a good reputation with agents, and much useful experience. It hardly felt like starting a new firm, more like carrying on the old one in improved conditions: we now had the equivalent of Bertie's and Roger's money without Bertie and Roger – just what we had longed for. This was so delightful that it might have relaxed some people's moral fibre, but not ours. Perhaps the most useful thing gained from Wingate was a disposition shaped by poverty. It had always been natural to André to be careful, and those who had worked with him at Wingate, seeing that his attitude was strictly necessary for survival, had fallen into it themselves – even those like me, whose natural tendency was towards extravagance. Since then I have often noticed that it is not good for people to start a venture with enough – not to mention too much – money: it is hard for them to learn to structure it properly, simply because they are never forced to.

Even if we had been eager to relax we would not have been allowed to. André felt it to be a danger. He countered it by putting up a blood-chilling front of gloom about our prospects for the next forty years. However well we were doing, the slightest hint that expenditure of some sort would not come amiss (the redecoration of the reception area, perhaps, or thirty-two pages of illustrations in a book instead of sixteen, or – God forbid – a rise for someone) would bring on a fit of shocked incredulity at such frivolous heedlessness in the face of imminent disaster. Much though the rest of us used to complain about this frugality, it is a fact that our firm continued to make a profit every year until he sold it in 1985, in spite of the last five years of that time being hard ones for small independent publishing houses; and this might not have been –

towards the end certainly would not have been – possible had his control of our overheads been less fierce.

For three years we rented the top two-thirds of a doctor's house in Thayer Street. They were happy years, but still a touch amateurish: did proper publishers have to put a board over a bath in order to make a packing-bench? Did proper editors and proper sales managers work together in the same small room? Our performance, nevertheless, was good enough to let us buy up Derek Verschoyle's firm in 1956, and move into its premises at 14 Carlisle Street in Soho.

Derek Verschoyle was a raffish figure, vaguely well-connected and vaguely literary, about whom I had first heard from my father who had encountered him as an agreeably picturesque feature of the *Spectator*. Verschoyle was its literary editor for a while. His room looked out over the mews behind that periodical's offices in Gower Street, and he, lolling with his feet up on his desk, used to take pot-shots at the local cats out of his window with a .22 which he kept on his desk for the purpose. He must have been able to raise a fair amount of money in order to set up his own publishing firm (its assets included the freehold of the house, which was very well placed) but it didn't take him long to get through it. We gained only two really valuable authors from him – Roy Fuller, whose novels and poetry added lustre to our list for a long time, and Ludwig Bemelmans, whose 'Madeline books' for young children did very well for us. One of the more burdensome books we inherited from him was a pointless compilation called *Memorable Balls*, a title so much tittered over that we thought of leaving it out when we were arranging our stand at *The Sunday Times*'s first book fair. Finally one copy was shoved into an inconspicuous corner – where the

Queen Mother, who had opened the fair, instantly noticed it. Picking it up, she exclaimed with delight: 'Oh, what a tempting title!' André insisted that it was his confusion over this that made him drop her a deep curtsey instead of a bow.

Verschoyle was the kind of English Gentleman André seemed fated to meet, but although undeclared liabilities went on leaking out of crannies for a long time, and the bills which came in with despairing regularity from his tailor and his wine merchant used to make our eyes pop, he did us no harm and much good. Settled into his house, we ceased being promising and became pros.

There were two large and well-proportioned rooms, and the rest of the house rambled back from its narrow frontage in a haphazard but convenient jumble of partitioned spaces. André, as was only right, had the better of the two good rooms, and Nick Bentley had the other. I moved fast to secure the smallest room there was, knowing that only the physical impossibility of inserting a second desk would save me from having to share. If I had put up a fight for Nick's room I would have got it, because Nick was far too well-mannered to fight back; but André would quite certainly have seen it as a chance to squeeze two other people into it with me, neither of whom would have been my secretary because I didn't have one. It never entered his head to ask Nick to share it with anyone other than his secretary.

Nick edited our non-fiction – not all of it, and not fast. He was such a stickler for correctness that he often had to be mopped-up after, when his treatment of someone's prose had been over-pedantic, or when his shock at a split infinitive had diverted his attention from some error of fact. I don't think I am flattering myself in believing that I was busier and more useful than he was (though there was nothing to choose between us in uselessness when it came to exercising business sense – a fact often bewailed by André, although he enjoyed the jokes he could make about it). I certainly noticed the privileges enjoyed by Nick as a result of his gender, just as I noticed that his salary was a good deal larger than mine; but what I felt about it was less resentment than a sort of amused resignation. All publishing was run by many badly-paid women and a few much better-paid men: an imbalance that women were, of course, aware of, but which they seemed to take for granted.

I have been asked by younger women how I brought myself to accept this situation so calmly, and I suppose that part of the answer must be conditioning: to a large extent I had been shaped by my background to please men, and many women of my age must remember how, as a result, you actually saw yourself – or part of you did – as men saw you, so you knew what would happen if you became assertive and behaved in a way which men thought tiresome and ridiculous. Grotesquely, you would start to look tiresome and ridiculous in your own eyes. Even now I would rather turn and walk away than risk my voice going shrill and my face going red as I slither into the sickening humiliation of undercutting my own justified anger by my own idiotic ineptitude.

But one can, of course, always walk away. That I could easily have done, and never thought of doing; so I doubt that it was *only* the mixed vanity and lack of confidence of the brainwashed female which held me there in acceptance of something which I knew to be unjust and which other women, whom I admired, were beginning actively to confront.

Some time in January 1998 I read in the *Independent* an article about recent 'research' (it sounded small-scale and superficial) into the differences between the attitudes of men and those of women towards their jobs. Men had been found more likely to aim for promotion and increased pay, women to aim for work they would enjoy and the satisfaction of doing it well. As so often when industrious people 'discover' something obvious, my first reaction was 'You don't say!'; but this was followed by an oddly satisfying sense of agreement, because the article did so exactly sum up my own experience. I hadn't just loved being an editor, I had also positively liked not being treated as the director I was supposed to be. This was because, as I have explained, I loathed and still loathe responsibility, am intensely reluctant to exert myself in any way that I don't enjoy, and am bored by thinking about money (in spite of liking to spend it). So while it is true that André took advantage of my nature in getting me cheap and having to bother so little about my feelings, it cannot be said that *in relation to the job* he did any violence to those feelings.

Obviously it is true that indifference to status and pay is not found in all women, but I have seen it in a good many who, like me, enjoyed their work. All my colleagues during the sixties and seventies admired and sympathized with other women who were actively campaigning for women's rights, but none of them joined in as campaigners: we could see injustice, but we didn't feel the pinch of it, because we happened to be doing what we wanted to do. Lazy or selfish? Yes, I suppose so. But I have to say that when I search myself for guilt about it – and guilt comes to me easily – I find none. While conditioning must have played some part in the inertia displayed by myself and my friends, my own experience suggests that it was at work on an innate disposition to be satisfied with my lot. After all, there are *some* men who mind more about enjoying their work than about what they are paid for it and where they stand in the hierarchy; so why, when a woman does the same, should it be taken for granted that she is brainwashed?

8

THE CARLISLE STREET years hummed with possibility. Although we had now been in the game long enough to know that the majority of manuscripts received would disappoint, we still expected excitement daily, and among the seventy-odd books a year that we published, a fair number justified that expectation. To Mailer, Richler, Moore and Fuller we soon added Terry Southern, V. S. Naipaul, Jack Kerouac, Philip Roth, Mavis Gallant, Wolf Mankowitz, Jack Schaefer, Jean Rhys – the poets Stevie Smith, Elizabeth Jennings, Laurie Lee, Peter Levi, Geoffrey Hill – the non-fiction writers Simone de Beauvoir, Peggy Guggenheim, Sally Belfrage, Alberto Denti di Pirajno, Lionel Fielden, Clare Sheridan, Mercedes d'Acosta (not all of them names likely to be recognized now, but all remarkable people who wrote remarkably well).

By now I considered myself a proper editor, so perhaps this is the place to describe the job as I saw it. In many firms a distinction was made between editors and copy-editors, the first being concerned with finding authors and keeping them happy, encouraging them in their projects and sometimes tempting them down this path or that; the second being the humbler but still essential people who tidy texts. In our firm a book's editor was responsible for both sides of the operation. Not until the eighties did we start farming out tidying jobs to free-lance copy-editors, and I doubt whether any Deutsch editor felt happy about doing so. I know I didn't.

The things which had to be done for all books were simple but time-consuming and sometimes boring (what kept one going through the boring bits was liking – usually – the book for which one was doing them). You had to see that the use of capital letters, hyphens, italics and quotation marks conformed to the house style and was consistent throughout; you had to check that no spelling mistakes had crept in, and make sure that if the punctuation was eccentric it was because the author wanted it that way; you had to watch out for carelessness (perhaps an author had decided halfway through to change a character's name from Joe to Bob: when he went back over the script to make the alteration, had he missed any 'Joes'?). You had to pick up errors of fact, querying ones you were doubtful about at the risk of looking silly. If your author quoted from other writers' work, or from a song, you had to check that he had applied for permission to do so – almost certainly he would not have done, so you would have to do it for him. If a list of acknowledgements and/or a bibliography and/or an index were called for you had to see that they were done. If the book was to be illustrated you might have to find the illustrations, and would certainly have to decide on their order and captioning, and see that they were paid for. And if anything in the book was obscene or potentially libellous you must submit it to a lawyer, and then persuade your author to act on his advice.

All that was routine, and applied to the work of even the most perfectionist of writers. Where the work became more interesting was when it was necessary to suggest and discuss alterations to the text.

Editorial intervention ranged from very minor matters (a clumsy sentence here, a slight lack of clarity there) to almost complete rewritings such as I did on the book about Tahiti (although I don't remember ever doing another rewrite as extensive as that one). Usually it would be on the lines of 'Wouldn't it work better if you moved the paragraph describing so-and-so's looks back to where he first appears?' or 'Could you expand a little on so-and-so's motive for doing such-and-such? It's rather arbitrary as it stands'. I can't remember anyone resenting such suggestions, though sometimes of course they would disagree for good reasons: mostly, if what is said by an obviously attentive reader makes sense, the writer is pleased to comply. Writers don't encounter *really* attentive readers as often as you might expect, and find them balm to their twitchy nerves when they do; which gives their editors a good start with them.

It was a rule with me that I must not overdo such tinkerings: it must always be the author's voice that was heard, not mine, even if that meant retaining something that I didn't much like. And of course it was an absolute rule with all of us that no change of any kind could be made without the author's approval. It was those two points which I considered my ground-rules. The ideal was to receive a script which could go through unchanged (Brian Moore, V. S. Naipaul and Jean Rhys were outstanding providers of such scripts; and books already published in America were equally trouble-free, because such editorial work as they had needed would have been done over there). If, on the other hand, the text had needed work, then by the time it reached publication it must read as though none had been done on it, which could usually only be achieved by working closely with the author.

Writers varied greatly in their attitude to intervention. I never came across anyone who was anything but grateful at having a mistake, whether of fact or syntax, pointed out, but when it came to changes some weighed every word of every suggestion, many accepted suggestions cheerfully, a few asked for more, and a very few didn't seem to care one way or another.

George Mikes, for example, needed a lot of work done on his books. He was a lazy man, one of those people who, once they have become fluent enough in a foreign language to say what they want, can't be bothered to go the step further which would enable them to say it correctly. If his writing was to sound like natural, easy-going colloquial English, which he was aiming for, about one sentence in every three had to be adjusted. For the first two or three of the thirteen of his books that I edited, he took the trouble to read the edited script, but gradually he paid it less and less attention until, with the last three of his books, he would not even glance at the script – not even when I told him that I had put in a couple of jokes! Knowing him very well, I always felt quite sure that I had made his books sound just like he would have sounded if he had pushed his English up that last notch – that he was, in fact, right to trust me: but still I was slightly shocked at his doing so.

One kind of editing I did not enjoy: cookery books. We built up a list which eventually amounted to over forty titles, mostly about national cuisines or the use of a particular ingredient – rice cooking, mushroom cooking, cooking with yoghurt and so on. This list was André's idea – he it was who saw that as food supplies returned to normal, thousands of the British middle class would for the first time have to cook it with their own hands. I was too uninterested in food to have thought of it: in those days my notion of adventurous cooking was scrambling an egg instead of boiling it. But I was a woman, and where was the woman's place but in the kitchen? So the cookery list became 'mine'.

Luckily André capped his first inspiration by meeting Elizabeth David at a dinner party and inviting her to become our cookery-book consultant, and her year or so of doing this saved me. Quickly she taught me to look for authenticity, to avoid gimmicks, to appreciate how a genuine enjoyment of food made a book tempting without any self-conscious attempts at 'atmosphere'. Before long I could see for myself that Elizabeth would never have done as the sole editor of a cookery-book list because so many useful books would prove too coarse to get through the fine sieve of her rather snobbish perfectionism; but her respect for the art of cooking and the elegant sensuousness of her response to flavour and texture were an education in the enjoyment of eating, as well as in the production of cookery books, for which I am still grateful.

There is no kind of editing more laborious than getting a cookery book right. You cannot assume that a procedure described in detail on page 21 will be remembered by a cook using a recipe on page 37 or 102: it must be fully described every single time it is used. And never can you be sure that all the ingredients listed at the head of a recipe will appear in their proper place within it. You must check, check and check again, and if you slip into working automatically, without forcing yourself to imagine actually *doing* what you are reading, you will let through appalling blunders (oh those outraged letters from cooks saying 'Where do the three eggs go in your recipe for such-and-such'!). I did become proud of our cookery list, and fond of some of its authors – but even so, cookery books ran advertisements close as my least favourite things.

I suppose that when I started on them I had never come across any description of the traditional savagery of great chefs: I assumed that people, many of them comfortably built and rosy-faced, who wrote about what was evidently to them a great sensuous pleasure, would be by nature mellow and generous. When a West End bookshop devoted a week to promoting cookery books, and accepted our suggestion that it should open with a party for which six of our cooks should provide the food, I expected a merry evening. The six joined eagerly in the preliminary planning, which had to ensure that each would bring two dishes suitable for finger eating, which represented her own speciality and which didn't clash with the other cooks' contributions. They bravely undertook the task of transporting their delicate work to the shop, and all arrived in good time to set about arranging the food to its best advantage. Whereupon – crunch! and someone's tray landed on someone else's plate – splat! and a passing rump sent a dish flying to the floor – 'Oh do let me help!' and a knife was seized and brought to bear like a jolly hockey stick on a rival's exquisite confection . . . Never again did I allow any of our cooks to meet each other.

The kind of cookery book we brought out in the fifties, and which continued to do well in only slightly modified form during the sixties and seventies, would not get far today. It was an inexpensive, unillustrated collection of recipes which we assumed would sell (and which did sell) without being dressed up, because many of the new generation of middle-class cooks were enjoying holidays abroad for the first time and were therefore eager to make their meals more interesting by cooking dishes from foreign countries. As Britain's culinary revolution progressed (and you only

have to look at a few of the cookery books published before the
Second World War to see that it was a real revolution), more publishers jumped on the bandwagon and more effort had to be put
into making cookery books eye-catching. It was a good many years
before the grand, glossy, lavishly illustrated tome swept the board,
but the challenge became perceptible fairly soon, and we failed to
rise to it.

Booksellers began to insist that they couldn't sell a cookery book
unless it was illustrated in colour, so reluctantly we started to insert
a few cheaply printed colour plates, the photographs usually
scrounged from a tourist board, which was a waste of time and of
the little money it cost. I knew this; it was obvious that the big suc-
cesses were crammed with beautiful photographs specially taken
for them and finely printed. They could only be so handsome
because their publishers had the confidence to invest a lot of money
in producing large editions, and printed their colour in even longer
runs for several foreign editions as well as their own. To work on
this scale they had to establish and cherish a Name – Carrier, Boxer
and so on – culminating today in Delia, Queen of the Screen (one
of the best things about cookery books is that no one who isn't a
truly good cook can become a Name, because recipes are *used*).
Then the book had to be planned so that the purchaser could feel
'That's it, I shall never need another!' (which didn't have to worry
the Name, because once solidly established, collections of his or her
Summer, Winter, Christmas, Birthday, Party or Whatever recipes
would still sell merrily, even though a critical eye might detect signs
of strain). Then photographers who could make food look eatable
had to be found – a much rarer breed than the uninitiated would
suppose, and worth their weight in caviare. And finally a network
of international relationships had to be built up. This kind of

investment was foreign to André's nature, and I certainly had not got the confidence to fight for it. Suppose we didn't get it right first time? We easily might not, and we could not afford such a disaster. So we settled for the modest success of our own kind of book, which slowly decreased until the early eighties, when the list faded out.

The stalest cliché about publishing – 'You meet such interesting people' – is true enough, but I think the greatest advantage it offers as a job is variety. Yes, I did find working on cookery books fairly boring, but how different it was from working on a novel or a book of poems. One was always moving from one kind of world into another, and that I loved.

I was nervous in the world of poetry. My mother used flatly to refuse to read it, declaring that it made no sense to her, and although I was shocked and embarrassed on her behalf in my teens, when I read poetry a good deal and wrote it too (though never supposing I was writing it well), I had in fact inherited her prosaic nature. Poetry moves me most sharply when it ambushes me from a moment of prose, and I can't really understand what it is that makes a person feel that to write it is his *raison d'être*.

Knowing this, all I could do while a volume of poetry was going through my hands was stand by – which, luckily, is all that an editor ought to do unless he is Pound working with Eliot: one poet rubbing sparks out of another in mutual understanding. I read the work carefully, tried to make the jacket blurb say what the author wanted it to say, was moved by some of the poems as wholes and by parts of other poems . . . all that was all right. But I also felt a kind of nervous reverence which I now find tiresome, because it was what I supposed one *ought* to feel in the presence of a superior being; and poets, although they do have a twist to their nature

which non-poets lack, which enables them to produce verbal arte-
facts of superior intensity, are not superior beings. In the distant
days when they were singing stories to their fellows in order to
entertain and instruct them, they were useful ones: in the days
when they devised and manipulated forms in which to contain the
more common and important human emotions they were clever
and delightful ones; and in the comparatively recent days when
they have examined chiefly their own inner landscapes they have
often become boring ones (I have stopped reading the
Independent's 'Poem of the Day' because of how distressingly uninteresting most of them are). And even when the poems are not
boring, the poet can be far from superior – think of poor Larkin!

Naturally we did not think the poets we chose to publish
boring – except that I did become tired of Roy Fuller's meditations
on his own ageing, sometimes found Elizabeth Jennings's thought
less interesting than she did, and considered that 'Not Waving But
Drowning' was the best-known of Stevie Smith's poems because it
was the best of them. Peter Levi's early poems I found easy to love,
but it was Geoffrey Hill's dense and knotty poems which were, for
me, the richest in sudden flashes and enduring illuminations. 'If
you are really without religious feelings,' he once said to me, 'how
can you like my work?' To which the answer is: 'Does an agnostic
have to dislike a Bach cantata or Botticelli's *Nativity*?' If an emotion
or a state of mind has forced someone to give it intensely appro-
priate expression, that expression will have power enough to bypass
opinion.

Geoffrey was a difficult writer to work with because of his anxiety: he was bedevilled by premonitions of disaster, and had to be
patiently and repeatedly reassured although my own nerves,
worked on by his, would be fraying even as I spoke or wrote my

soothing words. Once something frightening happened. A book of his – I think it was *Mercian Hymns* – had been read in page-proof by him and me, and I had just passed it to the production department to be sent to press. That same afternoon he telephoned apologetically, saying he was aware of how neurotic he was being and would I please forgive him, but he had suddenly started to worry about whether the copyright line had been included in the preliminary pages. I knew it had been, but I also knew how tormenting his anxieties were, so instead of saying 'Yes, of course it's there,' I said: 'Production probably hasn't sent it off yet, so hold on and I'll run down and check so that we can be a hundred per cent sure.' Which I did, and the line was there, and Geoffrey was comforted. And when the printed book was delivered to us there was no copyright line.

Whatever it may be that causes a poet to know himself one, Geoffrey was walking evidence of his own sense of vocation. Living seemed to be more difficult for him than for most people. Once he told me – wryly, not proudly – that he was hesitating about doing something which he passionately wanted to do because if he did it, and thus ceased to suffer, he might never write any more poems. And his prose seemed to illustrate the degree to which writing poetry was his *raison d'être*: it was so unconfident and clumsy that it made me think of a swan out of water.

Stevie Smith, too, in her different way, found life difficult; although she solved the problem cleverly and decisively by withdrawing from those parts of it that were too much for her and keeping to a well-defined territory of her own. She was amusing, and – strangely, given the cautious nature of her strategy – met one with a beguiling openness, so that I always started our meetings with the feeling that we were about to become close friends. We

never did, and I think the reason was sexual. I was still young
enough to be at heart more interested in my own sexual and
romantic activities than in anything else (though mostly I kept
them out of my office life), so Stevie's nervous asexuality distanced
her. She almost fainted when she first came into my office, because
I had on my wall a print of snakes. All the blood left her face and
she could hardly make audible a plea that I should take the print
down (after that I always removed it as soon as she was
announced). Perhaps the notion that a phobia about snakes relates
to their phallic quality is old-fashioned and misguided, but I supposed it to be true, and saw Stevie's phobia as revealing. I'm sorry
to say that some part of me slightly despised the fear of sex I sensed
in her; and I hope that she got her own back (this is far from
unlikely) by slightly despising its opposite quality in me.

That we had a poetry list was almost accidental. While we were
still at Thayer Street André had met Laurie Lee and had fallen in
love with his *Cider with Rosie*, which was published by Chatto &
Windus. Laurie must already have been dabbling in the manipulative games with publishers that he was to play with increasing zest in
the future, because André was given to understand that Chatto's
were in the dog-house for refusing to publish his poems, *My Many-
Coated Man*, and who knew what might come the way, in the
future, of the firm which took them on. So André snapped up the
poems (and we did indeed get Laurie's next-but-one prose book).
Six months later the acquisition of Derek Verschoyle's list landed us
with five more books of verse. They were by Ronald Bottrall, Alan
Ross, Roy Fuller, Diana Witherby and David Wright – Fuller was to
continue with us for the next thirty years. Then Elizabeth Jennings
came to us on Laurie's recommendation, and Peter Levi on
Elizabeth's, and after that one poet led to another in a haphazard

way, or sometimes an agent bobbed up with one, or sometimes one of our novelists was a poet as well (notably John Updike), and once there was a small infusion from another publisher, called Rapp & Whiting, whose list came our way . . .

In the almost fifty years I spent in publishing, poetry was never easy to sell, and we were not among the houses that were best at it. I find it hard to understand why we stayed with it as long as we did. Certainly I loved some of the books on our poetry list, but given my prosaic nature I would not have minded if we had never developed such a list: I edited most of the books on it, but I was not its instigator. It was André who liked to have it there. He had been an enthusiastic reader of poetry in his youth (Hungarians treasure their poets very earnestly), and was still, when I first knew him, reading Eliot's *Four Quartets* aloud to young women whenever they gave him the chance (and reading them well). Nor was Nick much interested in our poets – except for Ogden Nash who was a friend of his, and whom he edited. I suppose André simply thought that a proper publisher had a poetry list, rather as, in the past, an English country gentleman, even if he devoted all his leisure to shooting game birds or riding to hounds, thought that a proper house had a library. In retrospect I see it as interesting rather than praiseworthy, given the frugal habits insisted on by André. Poetry may not have lost us money (we paid poets minuscule advances and designed their books very economically), but it certainly didn't make us any, and none of us minded: an attitude which fifty – forty – thirty years ago was not worthy of remark, and now has become almost unimaginable.

To restore my balance after recalling the dutiful aspects of editing – the need to work conscientiously in spite of being bored, and to put oneself at the service of books that were not always within one's range – I shall now describe what was certainly the most absorbing of all the tasks that came my way: working with Gitta Sereny on *Into That Darkness*, which we published in 1974.

Gitta spent her childhood in Vienna, the daughter of a Hungarian father and an Austrian mother, neither of them Jewish. She was fifteen years old when Hitler took Austria over. She was sent to school in France and was caught there by the war. During the German occupation she looked after abandoned children in Paris and the Loire, then got out to America where, in 1945, she took a job in UNRRA (the United Nations Relief and Rehabilitation Administration) as a child welfare officer in camps for displaced people in southern Germany. Although many of the children were eventually reunited with their families, many more had no one and nowhere to go to: all had experienced unspeakable horrors. How could anyone have chosen to make concentration-camp and labour-camp victims of thousands of children, all under fourteen, many under ten? To quote from the preface to the first paperback edition of *Into That Darkness* which we published in 1991: 'Over the months of the Nuremberg trials and our own increasing work with survivors, including a few from the extermination camps in occupied Poland, about which almost nothing had been known until then, we learnt more and more about the horrors which had been committed, and I felt more and more that we needed to find someone capable of explaining to us how presumably normal human beings had been brought to do what had been done.' Haunted by this question, she came to feel that 'it was essential to penetrate the personality of at least one such person who had been intimately associated with this total evil. If it could be achieved, an evaluation of such a person's background, his childhood, and eventually his adult motivation and reactions, as he saw them, rather than as we wished or prejudged them to be, might teach us to understand better to what extent evil in human beings is created by their genes, and to what extent by their society and environment.'

People sometimes ask why Gitta Sereny habitually writes about evil, but I do not see it as surprising that someone plunged into such a scalding awareness of it so early in her life should be haunted by it. It is only because it frightens us too much that we don't all think about it much more than we do. Everything that makes life worth living is the result of humankind's impulse to fight the darkness in itself, and attempting to understand evil is part of that fight. It is true that such understanding as has been achieved has not made much – if any – headway against evil; and it is equally true that horror and dismay at dreadful things are often used as disguise for excitement; but if those facts are allowed to discourage us from trying to understand how corruption comes about, what hope have we? It seems to me that Gitta's need to seek explanations has led her to do valuable work, none more so than when she seized the chance, some twenty-five years after her experiences in UNRRA, to penetrate one particular evil personality.

She had become a journalist. In 1967 she was commissioned by the *Daily Telegraph* to write a series of pieces about West Germany, including the Nazi crime trials then taking place. She was present at the trial of Franz Stangl who had been Kommandant of Treblinka, one of the four extermination (as opposed to concentration) camps in German-occupied Poland, and who was sentenced to life imprisonment for co-responsibility in the murder of 900,000 people in that camp. There had been only four such men: one of the others was dead, the other two had escaped. Stangl, too, had escaped (to

Brazil), but had been tracked down. Gitta realized that he was the object for study that she had hoped for, and that by now she herself felt capable of undertaking the task.

She was allowed to visit Stangl in prison and talked with him for many hours over six weeks, at the end of which – the very end – he reached the bottom of his guilt and admitted that he ought not still to be alive. There was still a detail which he wished to confirm about something he had said, so she agreed to return to the prison in three days' time to collect the information. When she did so she was told that he was dead. It had been heart failure, not suicide. When the *Telegraph Magazine* published the interviews they refused to include this fact, saying that no one would believe it.

Having read these interviews, we asked Gitta to come to the office and discuss the possibility of a book, whereupon she told us that she was already deep in the work for it, and would be glad to let us see it. I can't remember how long it was before she brought it in – or rather, brought in the raw material out of which it was to be shaped, but I shall never forget the sight of that mountain of script.

When I got it home that evening (it was far too unwieldy to deal with in the office) it covered the whole of my table. In addition to the central Stangl interviews there were interviews, many of them long, with at least twenty-four other people, and there was also much – though not all – of the material for the linking passages of description and explanation essential to welding the material into a whole.

No reading I have ever done has shaken me as much as the reading I did that night. Having seen the film of Belsen made when the Allies got there I thought I knew the nature of what had been done; but of course I didn't. Groping my way into the history of this ordinary, efficient, ambitious, uxorious Austrian policeman, through the astonishing material about Hitler's euthanasia programme to which he was transferred – all the men employed in the extermination camps, except for the Ukrainians, worked for that programme – was intensely interesting, but frightening because I knew where it was going. And then it got there. And then the voices began to tell me what it had really been like . . . I remember walking round and round the room as though I were trying to escape what was in that pile of paper, and I didn't sleep that night. But one editorial decision I was able to make then and there: we must use no adjectives – or very few. Words such as 'horrifying', 'atrocious', 'tragic', 'terrifying' – they shrivelled like scraps of paper thrown into a blazing fire.

After the enormous amount of source material she had dug into, and all those interviews which had taken her to Brazil and Canada and the United States as well as to Germany and Austria, and had plunged her ever deeper into the darkness that I had just glimpsed, Gitta was near the end of her tether. She liked to have the support of an editor at the best of times, simply because, fluent though her English was, it was not her first language: she couldn't be absolutely confident in it – and did, in fact, sometimes slip into slightly Germanic rhythms and over-elaboration of syntax. But chiefly it was exhaustion, and being too close to the material, which made it essential for her to have help. Often it amounted to no more than me saying 'Let's put that bit here' so that she could say at once 'No no – it must go there'; but she was also enabled to reshape passages when she had seen them afresh through a new pair of eyes. I could point out where clarification, condensation, expansion were needed. I could say 'But you've said that already when you were

describing such-and-such', or 'But wait a minute – I need reminding about that because it was so long ago that it first came up'.

It was clear enough that the Stangl interviews were the thread on
which the rest must hang, but it was not easy to decide where to
break them and introduce other voices: his wife's or his sister-in-
law's, those of the men who worked under him, those of the five
survivors, and many more. I have forgotten how long it took us,
working usually in my flat (I had to take many days away from the
office for this book); but I know it was months – Gitta often had to
go back to her typewriter to provide links or expansions. From
time to time we got stuck: there would be a chunk of material, fascinating in itself but seemingly impossible to fit in. 'Oh God, we'll
just have to sacrifice it', I would say; and then, a little later, there
would be some slight shift in the mass of the book, and click! in
would go the problem piece, fitting exactly. This happened with
almost uncanny regularity. Gitta *thought* she had just been collecting everything she could find, but the extent to which she had
unconsciously been structuring her book became clearer and
clearer. An interviewer does, after all, control the direction of an
interview, and the further she had delved into Stangl's background,
the more sure her touch had become at discovering what was rel-
evant. We shortened a good deal, but we did not, in the end, have to
leave anything out.

That was the most impressive thing about her work on this
book: the way she knew, even when she felt as though she didn't,
exactly what, in this most complicated operation, she was after.
That, and her astonishing power as an interviewer which enabled
her to draw out of people all that they had to give. And another
thing which won my admiration was her lack of author's vanity.
She would sometimes say 'no' to an alteration I suggested, on the

grounds that it sounded too unlike her; but usually if a point were made **more** concisely or emphatically she appeared not to mind if I altered **her** original words. What she was committed to was *getting things said* rather than to making an impression as a wordsmith.

I could write at length about *Into That Darkness*, but it would make more sense for **those** of my readers who don't know it to get hold of a copy. The **reason** why working on it was so important to me was that its subject **engaged** me so completely. I still think – and often – of how that **unremarkable** man became a monster as the result of a chain of choices between right and wrong – some of the early ones quite trivial – **and the** way in which no one he respected intervened in favour of **the** right, while a number of people he respected (senior officers, a priest, **a** doctor – his idea of respectability was conventional) behaved as though the wrong were right. Chief among them, of course, the Führer. Stangl did not have a strong centre – had probably been deprived of it by a dreary childhood – so he became a creature of the **regime**. Other people without much centre didn't – or not to the same **extent** – so some quality inherent in him (perhaps lack of imagination combined with ambition) must have been evident to those **who** picked him for his appalling jobs. But it was surely environment **rather** than genes which made him what he became.

One good thing about being old is that one no longer minds so much about what people think of one. Boasting is disapproved of, but still I am going to quote the words with which Gitta acknowledged my help, because they gave me so much pleasure: 'Diana Athill edited *Into That Darkness*. She has lent it – and me – her warmth, her intelligence, her literary fluency, and a quality of involvement I had little right to expect. I am grateful that she has become my friend.' Which makes us quits, because I was and am grateful to my friend Gitta for allowing me that involvement.

Soon after the book was finished Gitta became ill: a cancer, discovered – thank God – early enough for complete extirpation. I know, of course, that there can be no proof of this, but I have always been convinced that it was a consequence of the strain she underwent when she had the courage to follow that man so closely into his dreadful night.

9

DOMESTIC LIFE AT Carlisle Street (and later) was as full of incident as professional life, and this was for two reasons: the first, André's weakness for the square peg; the second, love.

The square pegs were many, often harmless and soon remedied, sometimes dramatic. Two were actually deranged, one of them a sales manager, the other put in charge of publicity (I was at last allowed to hand over the advertising to a publicity department, such an overpowering relief that it was some time before I could believe it, and rejoice). The sales manager, who had been imported from Australia, was living in a hotel, and I remember going there with André, hoping to find out why he hadn't appeared at the office for three days, and being told by the receptionist in a hushed voice, as if he were divulging the movements of a celebrity: 'The Colonel left for Berlin two days ago.' The *Colonel*?? We were never to find out more about his attack of military rank, nor about his disappearance. The publicity lady simply suffered from *folie de grandeur*, which provided its own solution when she realized that the job was beneath her.

The square peg I remember most fondly I shall call Louise.
André found her in New York, writing copy for Tiffany's catalogue,
and saw in a flash that she was just the person to manage the editorial department: not to do editing, but to *organize the editors*. He
had long nursed a dream of programming and wall-charts which
would somehow overcome the hazards which beset a book's
progress from typewriter to printing press: authors having second
thoughts, indexers going down with 'flu, holders of copyright not
answering letters and so on. Louise was going to cure him of this
dream, but we were unable to foresee the happy outcome, and
awaited her arrival with dread. He had announced her thus: 'You
are all going to have to *obey* her absolutely. Even *I* am going to
obey her.'

She did at first sight seem a little alarming – but only because she
was so chic. She was willowy and fine-boned, and her clothes were
almost painfully enviable: the sort of casual clothes at which classy
New Yorkers excel, so simple that you can't pinpoint why you know
they are very expensive, you just do know it. But her striking poise
and confidence did not prevent her manner from being engaging,
so I took her to lunch on her first day feeling warmer towards her
than I had expected; and indeed, we had not finished the first
course before every trace of alarm had been dispersed.

Louise couldn't wait to tell me why she had accepted André's
offer. She had met Ken Tynan in New York (Tynan was even more
famous there, both as theatre critic and as personality, than he was
in London); she had fallen madly in love with him; when he had
left for London she had been flat broke (*how did she get those
clothes?*) so that she couldn't possibly follow him, and had been in
despair . . . and then, out of the blue, came this God-sent chance.
Did I think Ken would mind? She was almost sure he wouldn't, he

had said this, that and the other, done this, that and the other . . .
Surely that must mean that their affair was about to go from
strength to strength . . . Or did I think, perhaps, that she had been
unwise? I had never been nearer Tynan than the far side of a room
at a drinks party, but it was impossible not to hear a great deal
about him, and what I had heard made me pretty sure that she had
been very unwise. I could already envisage mopping-up operations
ahead, but what chiefly occupied my mind on that first day was the
cheerful certainty that this charming but daft girl was never going
to manage anything, not even her doomed love-life.

What still remained to be discovered was the extent of her curi-
ously vulnerable recklessness – her almost heroic compulsion to
plunge into disaster – and her total uselessness in an office. She was
a brilliant con-artist as far as the first moves went – that first
impression of exceptional poise and confidence never failed – but
she couldn't follow through. I don't think she even tried to. I came
to know her quite well, even had her to stay in my flat when her
need to be rescued became acute, and often wondered how well she
knew herself. Did she wake at night and start sweating at the
thought of being found out, or did she simply blank out awkward
facts such as that she had conned her way into a job she couldn't do
and was now lying in her teeth to hide the fact that she wasn't
doing it? Blank them out, and then switch on some kind of instinctive escape mechanism by which she would wriggle out of this
situation and into another?

Not until she had left us did we discover that she had been
hiding book-proofs behind a radiator instead of sending them out,
as she had said that she had done, to distinguished persons in the
hope that they would provide glowing quotes to go on book-
jackets; but we did realize quite soon that when Louise said she had

done something it didn't necessarily mean that she had, and it was only a matter of weeks before André was muttering and rumbling – though not to her. He was rarely able to sack a square peg. His method was to complain about them angrily to everyone from Nick and me to our switchboard operator (never, of course, admitting that he had brought the offender in) until he had created such a thick miasma of discomfort in the office that even the most obtuse peg would sense that something was amiss, and would eventually leave. (On one appalling, and unforgiven, occasion, much later, when a peg had failed to do this, André broke down, gulping: 'I can't – I *can't* – *You* do it!' And I had to.)

Luckily Louise had sensitive feelers and soon became aware that thin ice was melting under her feet. So when one evening she found herself next to Tom Maschler of Cape's at a dinner party, she switched on her act. And a few days later Tom called André to apologize for having done a wicked thing: he had poached our Louise! 'I hope to God,' said André, 'that I wasn't *too* gracious about it.' Luckily Tom suspected nothing, and that was that. I went on seeing Louise from time to time, but thought it better not to ask her about her new job – it was her love-life that I was following. She finally accepted rejection by Tynan, embarked on a therapeutic flutter with a man who didn't interest her at all, became pregnant by him, and had an excuse to flee back to New York just in time – or so I suspected – to avoid being sacked.

I didn't say to André 'I told you so' because I knew so well, by then, that it would have no effect whatsoever.

The love which most disturbed the office – this was both surprising and gratifying – was that which afflicted men, not women. Among people of my grandparents' generation and, to a slightly lesser extent, my parents' it was taken for granted that men were to be preferred to women in responsible jobs because they were in better control of their emotional lives. A woman might be as intelligent as a man, but her intelligence could not be relied on because if, for instance, she was crossed in love she would go to pieces. Menstrual moodiness was not actually mentioned, but the idea of it lurked: women, poor things, were so designed that they couldn't be expected to overcome their bodies' vagaries. To my generation this was not true, but it was still present as something which needed to be disproved. I was therefore delighted to find that while I and my woman colleagues at work sometimes endured gruelling emotional experiences in our private lives, we none of us ever allowed them to impinge on our work in anything like the shameless way that Nick and André did.

Nick, usually a pattern of gentlemanly reticence with an upper lip so stiff that it almost creaked, fell violently in love with a young woman who was working for us, and by the time he had left his wife, forced her into divorcing him, been dumped by his mistress, and returned to his wife, the amount of hysteria that had been unleashed left the onlookers prostrate with exhaustion. At the stage when Nick was alone in a dreary rented flat soon after his woman had decided that she didn't want him after all, I felt truly sorry for him: a man so dignified having been reduced to making such a pathetic exhibition of himself, and all for nothing – it was tragic. But his dignity and my sympathy were a good deal reduced when, less than a week later, André reported that Nick was back with his wife and that we were all being asked to behave as though nothing had happened. I couldn't see any explanation for such a rapid anti-climax other than an inability to imagine life without being cooked, cleaned and shopped for.

André's love trials, less severe than Nick's but no less hard on the audience, were incidental to a story which turned out to be life-long and – with ups and downs – happy.

Earlier, at the time when I first became his confidante, he used to get through women very quickly. There would be an earnest report of falling in love (it was always love, never liking, that he fell into), soon followed by the news that it was over. On one occasion only three days passed between the falling and the revelation that the woman was impossible because 'she keeps on telephoning'. 'But isn't that rather nice?' I asked. 'No, she wants to talk about her troubles.' Another time he invited someone he had just met to share a short holiday in Cornwall, only to see next day that this was a mistake; whereupon he bullied Sheila Dunn to go with them and she in turn had to bully him not to lock the girl out of his bed-room – a situation I remembered on reading in Liane de Pougy's *My Blue Notebooks* how an ex-lover of hers summoned her to his rescue because a new flame had trundled into his bedroom equipped with her pillow, obviously expecting (*quelle horreur!*) to stay in his bed all night.

This flightiness was soon to change. In 1949 André went on the first of the skiing holidays in Davos which he was to take every winter for the rest of his active life, asking me before he left to look after his latest girl. I spent an evening with her – and it seemed to me that she showed no sign of infatuation, which was lucky. As soon as André got home he called me, to announce: 'I'm in love!'

'I know you are – you left me in charge of her.'

'Not with *her*. This is the real thing.'

And it was. Staying at the same hotel in Davos was the woman who would put an end to his days of philandering.

Her dark-haired brown-eyed beauty was of the slightly sharp-featured kind which most excited him, so it was not surprising that she had appealed to him on sight, but why she was the one who caught him for keeps – and it was obvious from the start that this had happened – is more mysterious.

I thought about it a lot, and came to the conclusion that four things had combined to give her the unshakeable authority she was to hold over his imagination: she was ten years older than he was, she was married, she was shy and reserved by nature and she was seriously rich.

Glamour requires a certain distance, and this beauty's seniority, her married status and her reserve endowed her with it: André would never be able to feel in complete possession of her. And her – or rather her husband's – money, which I am convinced André never thought of as something from which he might profit, enhanced this slightly out-of-reach glamour a good deal – and did so all the more effectively because she herself made very little of having money. She was gloriously special in André's eyes less for her amazing richness than because she was *above* her amazing richness.

At first he longed to marry her and felt, when her husband made this impossible, that they were in a tragic plight. But they were able to go on seeing each other, and finally he seemed to become resigned to the situation. He was in fact far too single-minded in his self-absorption to be good at marriage, however sincerely he would have adored his wife, and no one could have spent many years of meeting him almost every day without seeing as much.

In almost fifty years I met his beloved no more than a couple of dozen times, because André insisted that she was fiercely jealous of me. To begin with that was not inconceivable – I was ten years younger than she was, shared his interests and was with him every weekday – but as the years passed it seemed less and less likely; and by the time he said it (as he did) to an eighty-year-old me of a ninety-year-old her, it had become no more than an automatic twitch of an ossified male vanity. The truth was more likely to be that she had no intention of being lumbered with her lover's hangers-on. I believe she never once met his mother (for which no one who knew Maria Deutsch would dream of blaming her).

In any relationship as long as theirs there are ups and downs, and twice during our Carlisle Street days André was overtaken by fits of jealousy. Neither time, as far as I could see, did he have good reason for it, though that was not from want of trying to find one. Because both times, in addition to collapsing into a melting jelly of woe, unable to think or talk for days on end about anything else ('How can you expect me to think about print-runs when *this* is going on?' – which was hard to take given the degree of commitment he demanded from everyone else), he devoted evening after evening to what he called 'driving round', which meant spying, and for 'driving round' he insisted on a companion. He would endlessly circle whatever restaurant he thought she might be dining at; and having failed to catch her coming or going would then drive up and down the street where his suspected rival lived, hoping (or dreading) to see her car parked on it. Which he never did. If he had I would have known, because although I soon went on strike about 'driving round' with him, finding it as disgusting as it was boring, and was succeeded by other reluctant attendants, I still had to hear a blow-by-blow account of every evening, together with all the other moaning.

Why did I feel that I must go on listening? Nowadays, of course, I would soon find a way of escaping from such a desperately boring ordeal, but at the time it seemed to me that listening was what friends are for ... which is, I suppose, true enough up to a point, and it is not easy to draw a line between a genuine need for sympathy and greedy self-indulgence. I could and did draw it, but still I felt that André couldn't help crossing that line so that I *must* bear with him. I remember a particularly violent spasm of impatience, and thinking 'Hang on, don't let it rip, if he knew what I'm really feeling how could our friendship survive?'.

And in fact it was to be given a rude shock – though by André's impatience, not mine.

At about the time when he was going through his paroxysms of jealousy, and just before Nick's debacle, I fell in love with a man who had the courage, when he realized what had happened, to tell me that he was unable to fall in love with me. Even then I was grateful for his honesty because experience had already taught me a good deal about broken-heartedness, and I knew that the quickest cure is lack of hope. If mistaken kindness allows you the least glimmer of hope you snatch at it and your misery is prolonged: but this man (this dear man whom I continued to like very much after I was cured) made it impossible for me to fool myself, so I was able to set about getting better without delay and in the end was left without a scar. But although the process was steady it was not quick, and for about a year I had nothing to take my mind off sadness but my work, so that my evenings were often desolate.

Those enjoyed by André, his beloved, Nick and his wife Barbara seemed, on the other hand, to be all that evenings should be. They made a foursome and went to theatres, concerts, exhibitions and movies together two or three times a week. 'I wish that they would sometimes ask me to go with them,' I thought on one particularly dreary evening; and went on to wonder if it would be importunate to suggest as much to André. It would go against the grain to do so because I had fallen into the habit of keeping my love troubles to myself – and perhaps that was why it had not occurred to him that I could do with cheering up. If he knew . . . and we were, after all, friends: think of all the listening I'd done to *his* love troubles; think of all that 'driving round' for heaven's sake! Surely after all that I could bring myself to confess that I was going through a bad time and that an occasional evening at the cinema with him and the others would be very welcome.

So I did – probably, after all the screwing up to it which had gone on, in a tiresomely self-conscious voice. And what he said, very crossly, was: 'Oh for God's sake! Don't be so sorry for yourself.'

10

IN 1961 WE BOUGHT 105 Great Russell Street, where the firm was to spend the rest of its days. André pounced on it less because we needed a bigger house, although we did, than because it came with Grafton Books, a small firm specializing in books on librarianship, which he felt would contribute a ballast of bread and butter to our list in the future. In our early days we used to look respectfully at Faber & Faber because, as André often pointed out, their distinguished list of literary books was supported by others less glamorous – I think there were references to books about nursing – and we all felt slightly worried by our own lack of such reliable 'back-list' material. The cookery list was an attempt to remedy this, and so was the Language Library, a series of books on the nature and history of language which the lexicographer Eric Partridge thought up for us, and which he edited first entirely, then in an advisory capacity, until his death. Grafton seemed a timely expansion of this policy, and its house was splendid: a decent though often-adapted Georgian building, which bore a plaque announcing

that the architect A. W. N. Pugin once lived in it, and which we saw
at first as huge. The street on which it stood was drab, catering for
the kind of tourist who, clad in anorak and trainers, is in pursuit of
culture; but the British Museum still looks out on it through its
noble gates and a screen of plane trees, bestowing enough dignity
to make it a good address for a publisher.

Here we settled down to enjoy the sixties which were, indeed,
good years for us; although they never seemed to me essentially different from any other decade. Perhaps they would have done if I
had been younger and still fully responsive to the pull of fashion,
but as it was I saw them as an invention of the media. Most of the
people I knew had been bedding each other for years without calling it a sexual revolution. Jean Rhys agreed, saying that people were
using drugs like crazy when she first came to London before the
First World War, the only difference being that the papers didn't go
on about it. But of course the fact that we now felt that we had finished recovering from the Second World War did make for
cheerfulness.

Because we had more space in which to accommodate more
people we began to feel less like a family and more like a firm. For
some time we stuck at twenty-four people, not counting packing
and dispatch which was always under a separate roof and functioned efficiently and happily in the hands of an earnest Marxist
and various members of his family (until the fatal day when André
caught the suddenly-fashionable Management Consultant bug,
after which they became less efficient, and unhappy). Then the
production department grew from two to three to four; publicity
and rights each managed to convince André that they needed a
secretary of their own; Pamela Royds, our children's books editor,
forced herself to confess that she really did *have* to have an extra

hand (long overdue, given the size and importance of her list) . . . By the time we reached full strength we were using windowless passages as rooms and every real room was subdivided to the limit. Because my little room looked out of a window on the house's quiet side I felt guiltily privileged. Poor Esther Whitby and the other three of the editorial department were, for several years, entombed in the cellar.

I often wondered whether other businesses above the level of sweated labour imposed on their personnel the degree of discomfort we got away with. The country seemed to teem with people, most of them young women, so eager to work with books that they would endure poverty and pain to do so: a situation which we certainly exploited. The only people paid salaries commensurate with the value of their labour were our sales manager, our production manager and our accountant – all usually married men who would very properly not have taken the job for less. The rest of us, in spite of mopping and mowing fairly steadily about our pitiful lot . . . well, we could have left but we did not, and the atmosphere was usually cheerful.

Since I was always down among the common people as far as salary was concerned (several women who came to work for us after 1962 had the sense to insist on pay higher than mine), I felt like one of the employed rather than one of the employers. We were well into the nineteen-seventies before I reached £10,000 a year and I was never to be paid more than £15,000 – though some time in the late seventies I did get a company car (I remember André failing to convince me that a *deux chevaux* had a lot of throw-away chic). By the time we reached Great Russell Street I was no longer even noticing the extent to which the title 'Director', applied to me, meant next to nothing. When it came to buying property, increasing or not increasing staff, deciding where our books should be printed and what people should be paid, André made no pretence of preliminary discussion with anyone: which I accepted, so long as I was listened to – as I was – about books.

In only one respect do I now regret my attitude. If I had instinctively felt myself to be a senior officer rather than one of the crew I would have kept André in better order: would, for instance, have said 'Nonsense, of course we must buy them proper chairs and desk lamps – and *so what* if they cost as much as the ones you have just bought for yourself'. Instead of which I just, like everyone else, put up with the junk available, thinking 'What a mean old bastard he is' with the reluctant resignation of one complaining about bad weather.

Grafton Books was a good thing as far as it went, but it did not go very far: we were mistaken in thinking that it and the Language Library would keep us in bread and butter should we ever hit hard times. Grafton was run for us by Clive Bingley (who was to buy it from us in 1981) with the support of a small advisory committee, and he tended it through a growth as vigorous as a narrow field allowed; but few people had less interest in the technicalities of librarianship than André, Nick and me, so Clive must often have felt unsupported. When André sold it to him I think it was because of lack of interest in it rather than because it was losing us money, but it certainly was not bringing in a missable amount. And similarly, the Language Library would probably have done much better if one of us had cared about linguistics (for my part, having brushed the fringes of the subject at Oxford, I had moved rapidly through ignorance to abhorrence). It remained respectable, but it was unadventurous: we might, after all, have become the British publishers of Chomsky, but no one even thought about it. We hung on to the Language Library until 1984, and when we shunted it off onto Basil Blackwell Ltd of Oxford no one in the house noticed that it had gone. The truth is that a specialized list, if it is to succeed, must be published by a specialist: someone who will bring to it the energy and enthusiasm that we put into the rest of our list. Grafton and the Language Library made a modest but real contribution to the golden glow of our best years, but by the time when we began to see rough weather ahead both of them, for lack of love, had become the kind of cargo that can be jettisoned.

The books that did well for us in the next thirty years were the books we liked – not, of course, that they were all liked equally, or all by all of us, but all of them more or less 'our sort of book'. Among the more conspicuous of our novelists (I put them in alphabetical order to disguise preference) were Margaret Atwood (her three earliest), Peter Benchley (all his novels, but *Jaws* was the one which struck gold), Marilyn French (two of her novels, but it was *The Women's Room* which counted), Molly Keane (her three last, *Good Behaviour* supreme among them), Jack Kerouac, Norman Mailer (up to and including *An American Dream*), Timothy Mo (his first two), V. S. Naipaul (eighteen of his books, including non-fiction), Jean Rhys (all), Philip Roth (his first two), and John Updike (up to and including the collection of essays, *Odd Jobs*).

There were a great many others, a few of which I have forgotten, many of which I enjoyed, some of which I loved – and I shall insert here a note to those readers who like to poke about in second-hand bookshops: if you come across any of the following, *buy them*:

Michael Anthony's *The Year in San Fernando*. Michael came

from a remote Trinidadian village. His mother was very poor, and when offered the chance to send her boy to work for an old woman in San Fernando, she couldn't afford to turn it down. So the ten-year-old was dispatched to a small provincial town which seemed to him a thrilling and alarming metropolis; and Michael's novel is based on this experience. It is a wonderfully true and touching child's-eye view of life.

John Gardner's *Grendel*. A surprising novel to come out of Tennessee, by the man Raymond Carver acknowledged gratefully as a major influence. It is the Beowulf story told from the monster's point of view. Having to read *Beowulf* almost turned me against Oxford, so when a New York agent offered me this novel I could hardly bring myself to open it. If I hadn't I would have missed a great pleasure – a really powerful feat of imagination.

Michael Irwin's *Working Orders* and *Striker*. Two of the best novels of British working-class life I know – particularly *Striker*, which is about the making and breaking of a soccer star.

Chaman Nahal's *Azadi*. A superb novel about a Hindu family's experience of the partitioning of India, which ought to be recognized as a classic.

Merce Rodoreda's *The Pigeon Girl*. An extremely moving love story translated from the Catalan, which reveals much about the Spanish civil war as ordinary, non-political people had to live it.

It must seem to many readers that if someone was lucky enough to publish Roth's first books and almost all of Updike's, those two writers ought to figure largely in her story, but they are not going to do so. We lost Roth early through lack of faith, although I still think it was excusable. He, even more than Mailer, was a writer whose fame preceded his work: when his very gifted little first novel, *Goodbye, Columbus*, crossed the Atlantic it was all but invisible for the haze of desirability surrounding it, so that no one doubted for a moment that we had made a valuable catch. Then came *Letting Go* which I thought wonderful, although I agreed with André that it was too long – not 'by a third', as he said, but still too long. So we asked each other whether we should raise the matter with Philip and agreed that it would be too dangerous; there was such a buzz going on about him, everyone was after him – annoy him and he would be gone in a flash. And anyway it would be difficult to cut because it was all so good – there was not a dead line in it. Much of that novel is dialogue and I got the impression that Philip's brilliance with dialogue had gone to his head: he had enjoyed doing it so much that he couldn't bring himself to stop. So we accepted the novel as it was and it didn't earn its advance. (Imagine my feelings when he said to me, several years later: 'The trouble with *Letting Go* is that it's far too long.') Then came a novel called *When She Was Good*, told from the point of view of a young woman from the Middle West, non-Jewish, who struck me as being pretty obviously Philip's first wife. I never talked to him about this book, so what I say here is no more than my hunch, but I thought 'This is an exercise – he is trying to prove to himself that he doesn't *have* to write as a Jew and a man'. And as I read I kept telling myself 'It must soon come alive – it must'. And it didn't.

So we thought 'No more silly money' and decided to calculate the advance on precisely what we reckoned the book would sell – which I think was four thousand copies at the best – and that was not accepted. As far as I know *When She Was Good* was not a success – but the next novel Philip wrote was *Portnoy's Complaint*.

This space represents a tactful silence.

John Updike, on the other hand, was never set up as a star and never disappointed. From a publisher's point of view he was a perfect author: an extremely good writer who knows his own worth but is also well-informed about the realities of the publishing and bookselling trades. And from a personal point of view he is an exceptionally agreeable man, interesting, amusing and unpretentious, who knows how to guard his privacy without being unfriendly. I like John very much, always enjoyed meeting him, and never felt inclined to speculate about whatever he chose to keep to himself, so I have nothing to say about him except the obvious fact that we would have been a *much* less distinguished publishing house without him.

The strangest of my Great Russell Street experiences came in the mid-eighties, and did not result in a book. David Astor, the then retired editor of the *Observer*, and Mr Tims, a Methodist minister who had been a prison chaplain and had acted as counsellor to Myra Hindley, wanted her to write a truthful account of her part in the 'Moors Murders'. Mr Tims's motive was that of a Christian believing in redemption through penitence: he wanted, as a man in his position ought to want, to see this woman save her soul by plumbing the darkest depths of her guilt. Whether David Astor was at one with him about the soul-saving I am not sure, but he was convinced that if she could get to the bottom of her actions it would provide information valuable to sociologists and psychologists.

Encouraged by these two men, she had written about her childhood and about meeting Ian Brady, falling in love with him and starting to live with him; but when she approached the murders, she stuck. She needed help. She needed an editor.

David Astor invited André and me to his house to meet Mr Tims and discuss the matter. It was soon after Tom Rosenthal had joined us, in the first stage of his buying the firm when he and André were to go through a period of joint management, so he too knew about the proposal. Our reactions to it had been characteristic: Tom's was instant and uncomplicated – he wouldn't touch anything to do with that monstrous woman with a bargepole; André's was uncomfortable but respectful, because he greatly admired David Astor and felt that any suggestion of his must be taken seriously; mine was a mixture of dismay and a curiosity too strong to be withstood. As we talked it over with the two men I became more and more sure that I wouldn't do it; but, having read the material they had persuaded her to write, I was ready to postpone my decision until after I had met her. She wrote simply and intelligently, making it clear how an ambitious nineteen-year-old with very little education, feeling herself to be more interesting than the rest of her family but frustratingly cut off from ways of proving it, could not fail to respond to the man she met at her work-place: the reserved austere man who quite obviously despised nearly everyone, but who *chose her*; who then went on to introduce her to frightening but fascinating books unknown to anyone else of her acquaintance; and who believed that it was necessary to be above the petty considerations which governed most people's despicable little lives. It was easy enough to see how that particular girl, falling in love with that particular man, would soon start to feel privileged, and to enjoy the sense of superiority gained by flouting ordinary people's timid limitations on behaviour. It was certainly not surprising that when she tried to confront the appalling results of following this line to its end, she couldn't. And I didn't see how anyone could help her do it – nor was I convinced that anyone ought to try. But given the chance to meet her, I was going to take it.

Mr Tims took me to the prison, a modern one, surrounded not by a wall but by a very high mesh fence. Its windows were of a normal size, out of which people could see grass and trees. Its only strangeness was that none of its inhabitants was visible: nobody was walking across those lawns or leaning out of those windows. No one but David Astor, André and Tom knew I was there – but I had not been in that prison fifteen minutes before a representative of a newspaper – I think the *Mail*, though I'm not sure – was on the telephone to the office asking if we were signing Myra Hindley up for a book. This, I was told later, always happened: wherever Hindley has been held, it seems there has been someone ready to keep the press informed of what is going on. To the British press, even after twenty-two years, Myra Hindley was firmly established as a kind of sacred monster, the least twitch of whose tail *had* to cause a ritual frenzy.

I spent about an hour with Myra Hindley, in a small room outside the open door of which sat a bored-looking wardress. If I had not known who the woman opposite me was, what would I have thought of her? I would have liked her. She was intelligent, responsive, humorous, dignified. And if someone had then informed me that this unknown woman had been in prison for twenty-two years I would have been amazed: how could a person of whom that was true appear to be so little institutionalized?

We talked about writing, of course – she had just taken a degree in English from the Open University – and about her conversion to Catholicism. She described how nightmarish it was to have the press breathing down the back of her neck all the time, and how boring to be short of intelligent talk. She was flippant rather than grateful about what she called 'my old men' – Lord Longford, David Astor, and Tims. To begin with her speech was very slightly slower than normal, so that I wondered if she was on tranquillizers – and Mr Tims was to say yes, she would have been: she had had to use them a lot since she had agreed to visit the moors with the police in an attempt to find the place where Brady had buried a victim whose remains had never been recovered. By the end of the hour she was speaking quite normally, and we could easily have gone on talking. I still liked her – and I had become quite sure that I was not going to become her editor.

The reason for this was two-fold: I could not believe that such a book would in fact teach anyone anything that could not already be inferred from the events, and I was also unable to believe that forcing herself to write it would help Myra Hindley. I was not a believer like Mr Tims, so about her soul I did not know: I was capable of envisaging the healing of guilt only in terms of *tout comprendre c'est tout pardonner*, and I did not think that this woman, if she compelled herself fully to acknowledge what she had done, would be able to grant herself pardon. When she did what she did, she was not mad – as Ian Brady was – and, although she was young, she was an adult, and an intelligent one. It seems to me that there are extremes of moral deformity which cannot be pardoned: that Stangl was right when, having faced the truth about himself, he said 'I ought to be dead'. He then had the luck to die, but that is not a conclusion that can be counted on. By the law of our land Myra Hindley had been condemned to live with what she had done, and she had contrived for herself a probably precarious way of doing so: admitting guilt, but blurring it by exaggerating her youth at the time and keeping the extent to which she had been influenced by, and eventually frightened by, Brady to the fore. What would society gain if she were made to live through those murders again as the sane adult she had in fact been, and ended by saying 'I ought to be dead', or by breaking down completely, which seemed to me the likely conclusion? Nothing. So if I enabled her to write the proposed book, and André Deutsch Limited published it, we would simply be trading in the pornography of evil, like the gutter press we despised. No, it could not be done.

Much of our non-fiction came in as a result of André's visits to New York: for example, John Kenneth Galbraith's books about economics, Arthur Schlesinger's about the Kennedy presidency, Joseph P. Lash's two about the Roosevelts. He also harvested many unexpected books such as Eric Berne's account of transactional analysis, *Games People Play*, very modish in its day, George Plimpton's funny stories about taking on professional sportsmen at their own games, and Helene Hanff's almost absurdly successful little collection of letters to a London bookseller, *84 Charing Cross Road*. Quickies by Daniel Cohn-Bendit and Bernadette Devlin resulted from his rapid response to whatever happened to be going on in the world; books by Gitta Sereny from his inability to read a newspaper without asking 'Is there a book in it?'. Simone de Beauvoir's books came from his flirtation with his old friend George Weidenfeld, with whom he had almost yearly meetings at which they discussed collaboration (sharing a warehouse, perhaps?), always to no avail except (mysteriously) in the case of joint publication of de Beauvoir. And it was André who launched us into our lively and profitable series of 'Insight Books' from *The Sunday Times*.

In the sixties Harold Evans made his name as the inspiring young editor of that paper, piloting it to the forefront of investigative journalism. His literary editor Leonard Russell, an old friend of Nick's and newer friend of André's, called André one day in 1967 to consult him about an offer the paper had just received. The Insight Team was doing an investigation of the Philby affair, it had occurred to them that there might be a book in it, and George Weidenfeld had offered £10,000: did André think this was about right? 'No,' said André. 'I will give you £20,000.' And that was that.

We had a slightly proprietorial feeling about Philby, because he had been introduced to us during his curious limbo-years between the defection of Burgess and Maclean to the Soviet Union and his own uncovering as a spy. Since 1949 Philby had been the top British Secret Intelligence Service man in Washington, liaising with the FBI and the CIA, and he and Burgess were colleagues both in their above-ground roles in the British secret service and in their underground roles as spies for Russia – he had even had Burgess to stay with him in Washington. He was therefore recalled to London for investigation and, although nothing could be proved against him, left his masters so uneasy that he was asked to resign. Soon afterwards a friend of Nick's, a rich picture dealer called Tommy Harris who had also been in the British Secret Service, came to us and suggested that we should commission Philby's life story: the poor man was now short of an occupation and of money, and of course there was nothing in the very unjust rumours which had followed his resignation. Tommy Harris brought him to meet Nick and André, who found him impressive and congenial, as did most of the people who met him, and who signed him up, agreeing to let him have his advance in instalments to keep him going during the writing. None of which was done, of course – I think Tommy Harris repaid the advance. Philby's failure to deliver was attributed to his finding, when he came to it, that he was not a writer. Another five years were to pass before the true reason emerged, on his disappearance to Russia. While it is possible for a dedicated professional spy to *live* a life of deceit – an effort constantly rewarded by the achievement of specific ends, and probably by the feeling that you are being cleverer than the enemy – it would be unutterably boring to *write* it: to slog away at a story completely lacking in the one element which gave it, from your point of view, meaning. Once Philby had 'come out' he was able to write what he felt to be the true story of his life very well.

There were to be five more 'Insight Books': a detailed analysis of a presidential election in America (Nixon's); a hair-raising account of how a financial colossus (Bernard Cornfeld) rose and fell; an over-view of the Middle Eastern war of 1973; the inside story of the Thalidomide disaster; and (the tail-end of the series, lacking the zing of its predecessors) *Strike*, the story of Thatcher, Scargill and the miners. All of them were team books produced by a group of exceptionally brilliant journalists in different combinations, chief among them Bruce Page, David Leitch, Phillip Knightley, Lewis Chester, Godfrey Hodgson and Charles Raw. The books emerged from a room at *The Sunday Times* so throbbing with activity that it was hard to imagine how a single paragraph of lucid prose could be written in it. It was Piers Burnett who edited them all for us, and he tells me that no experience in his long and varied publishing career was more entertaining.

In spite of André's record as a collector of square pegs, he did, of course, hit on many more round ones, and Piers was probably the roundest of them all. I think he was taken on as another attempt to impose on the editorial department that illusory orderliness and method of which André still spasmodically dreamt, and Piers did continue to function as an editor all the time he was with us; but quite soon his practicality, good sense and astonishing appetite for hard work got through to André. He had long nursed another dream in addition to that of the Editorial Manager; the dream of a Right Hand Man who would relieve the weight on his own shoulders by taking on at least some of the planning, negotiating and calculating with which he was burdened. He had recently made two attempts to bring this dream person in from outside, neither of which had worked – and very few of his onlookers would have been prepared to bet so much as a penny on any such attempt working. But now it dawned on him that perhaps what he needed was already in the house. He hesitated; he seemed for a while to be almost disgruntled at the prospect of anything so *easy*; and then the decision was made and Piers moved downstairs to the little room next to André's, and there, at last, was the Right Hand Man who suited possibly the most difficult man in London.

The most spectacular thing that Piers did for us was to bring in Peter Benchley's *Jaws* on his first visit to New York; but he was not ordinarily much at home with fiction, and when from '79 to '81 a small list under his own imprint came out under our wing it specialized in psychology and sociology. Nowadays his own publishing firm, Aurum Press, which he runs with Bill McCreadie (once our sales manager) and Sheila Murphy (once our publicity manager), has a much wider focus but still avoids fiction. Otherwise it is the nearest thing going to a 'Son of Deutsch': much nearer than the firm which now bears our name.

*

An aspect of our activities which seemed in the sixties to be very important was André's adventures in Africa. In '63 we declared: 'We are proud to announce that we are working in close association with AUP (African Universities Press, Lagos), the first indigenous publishing house in free Africa, the foundation of which was announced in Lagos in April this year. The greater part of AUP's output will be educational books chosen to answer the needs of Nigerian schools and colleges. It will, however, have a general list as well. Books on this list likely to appeal to readers outside Nigeria will be published simultaneously by us.' Two years later a similar announcement was made about the East African Publishing House in Kenya. Both publishing houses were started by André, who had chased up the local capital and editorial board for them and had found them each a manager. As a result we secured some good African novelists (my own favourites were *The Gab Boys* by Cameron Duodu and *My Mercedes Is Longer than Yours* by Nkem Nwankwo), and a number of intelligent books about African politics and economics – and André enjoyed some exciting trips. (One of them was too exciting. Meeting a seductive young woman at a party, he took her for a midnight stroll on a beautiful beach near Lagos, and they were hardly out of his hired car before he was flat on his face in the sand being knelt on by two large ragged men with long knives who slit his trousers pocket to get his wallet and car-keys, and might well have slit *him* if another large ragged man had not loomed out of the darkness to intervene. The thieves fled, the young woman was in hysterics, they were miles from the city centre or a telephone . . . all André could do was ask their rescuer to lead them to the nearest police station – at which all three of them were instantly arrested and the policemen started beating up the poor rescuer. It took André four hours to get the facts into the heads of the Law and procure a lift back to town – having not a penny left on him he couldn't offer a bribe. Nor could he give his rescuer a reward. He delivered the reward to the police station next day but was pretty sure it would not be passed on.)

Most of his African experiences, however, were pleasant and productive, and I admired him for having taken the current interest among publishers in the newly freed countries a step further than anyone else. Most of the people in our trade were more liberal than not, feeling guilty at being subjects of an imperial power and pleased that with the war's end Britain began relinquishing its so-called 'possessions' overseas. And many of them were genuinely interested in hearing what writers in those countries had to say now that they were free. For a time during the fifties and early sixties it was probably easier for a black writer to get his book accepted by a London publisher, and kindly reviewed thereafter, than it was for a young white person.

There was, of course, something else at work as well as literary and/or political interest. There are, after all, a vast number of Indians, Africans and West Indians in the world – a potential reading public beyond computation – and nowhere, except in India on a tiny scale, were these masses able to produce books for themselves. Certainly no British publisher was foolish enough to suppose that more than a minuscule fringe of that great potential market was, or would be for years, accessible, but I think most of us thought it would become increasingly accessible in the foreseeable future. The feeling in the air was that freedom would mean progress; that the market out there was certainly going to expand, however slowly, so that it would not only be interesting to get in on the ground floor of publishing for and about Africa: it would also prove, in the long run, to be good business. Longman's and

Macmillan's, with their specialized educational lists, were the firms which addressed the situation most sensibly, in ways helpful to their customers and profitable to themselves. André was the one who did it most romantically. Instead of providing Nigeria and Kenya with books made in Britain, he felt, Britain should help them develop publishing industries of their own. André Deutsch Limited was a shareholder in both the African houses he got off the ground, but not a major shareholder; and it claimed no say in what they were to publish. It was a generous enterprise, which seemed for a while to work well in a rough and ready way . . .

History, alas, has not left many traces of it, nor of the often wise and persuasive thinking in the non-fiction books about African affairs, particularly those of the French agronomist René Dumont, which we were so proud of. In Tanzania Julius Nyerere ordered a copy each of Dumont's *False Start in Africa* for every member of his government. He might as well have tossed them into Lake Victoria. But in the sixties it would have felt not only defeatist, but *wrong*, to foresee that the dangers Dumont warned against were not to be avoided.

Now I wonder whether we were expecting history to move faster than it can because we were witnesses of how fast an empire can crumble, and did not stop to think that falling down is always more rapid than building up . . . and what, anyway, were we expecting the multitude of tribal societies in that continent, many of them with roots more or less damaged by European intrusion, to build up *to*? Perhaps our concern was, and is, as much an aspect of neo-colonialism as American investment in Nigerian oil-wells.

André, and to some extent Piers, were the people who dealt with the African houses. My only brush with them came when we published a book by Tom Mboya jointly with EAPH and he came to

London for its launching. For some reason André was prevented from meeting him at the airport. Feeling that it would be rude just to send a limousine for him, he asked me to go in his stead. I had a clearer idea than he had of the value a Kenyan VIP would attribute to a middle-aged female of school-marmish appearance as a meeter, but André pooh-poohed my doubts and feebly I gave in. The drive from Heathrow to Mboya's hotel was even less agreeable than I expected. Almost all of it was spent by him and his henchmen discussing, with a good deal of sniggering and in an extemporized and wholly transparent code, how and where they were going to find fuckable blondes. But that little incident did not prevent me from feeling pleased about our African connection, seeing it as adding stature to our house.

Although I did not get to Africa, I did to the Caribbean: the only 'perk' of my career, but such a substantial one that I am not complaining. Among our several Caribbean writers was the prime minister of Trinidad & Tobago (two islands, one country), Eric Williams, with his *Capitalism and Slavery* and *From Columbus to Castro*. Such editorial consultation as was necessary could easily have been done by letter, but André delighted in collecting freebies. He saw journeys as a challenge, the object of the challenge being to get there without paying. At a pinch he would settle for an upgrading rather than a free flight – or even, if he was acting on someone else's behalf, for an invitation into the VIP lounge; but he was not often reduced to spending the firm's money on an economy fare. Acting on someone else's behalf gave him a cosy feeling of generosity, so when Eric Williams's proofs came in he staggered me by suggesting that I should take them to Port of Spain, and he wangled the works out of Eric: VIP lounge, first class, and free. I

had to get to New York on the cheapest charter flight I could find
(quite a complicated and chancy business in those days), but from
New York to Port of Spain it was champagne all the way. And once
there, after a short session with that aloof, almost stone-deaf man
whose only method of communication was the lecture, I could
extend the visit into a holiday.

And even that was free to begin with, because we were doing a
book about the islands for tourists, and the owners of the biggest
hotel on Tobago, confusing the word 'publishing' with 'publicity',
invited me to stay there. It was a luxurious hotel, but the people
staying in it were very old. The men played golf on its lovely links
all day, the women sat by its swimming-pool, apparently indifferent to the emerald and aquamarine sea being fished by pelicans a
stone's throw away, and the 'tropical fruit' announced on its menus
turned out to be grapefruit. I retired to my pretty cabin in a gloomy
state – and became much gloomier when I read the little notice on
the back of the door listing the hotel's prices. I did know, really, that
I was there as a guest, but it had not been put into words, and the
question 'Supposing I'm not?' seized on my mind. If I wasn't I'd
have to be shipped home in disgrace as an indigent seaman (when
I was a child my father told me that that was what consuls did to
people who ran out of money abroad). So next morning I took to
the bush with that irrational worry still gnawing, and had the luck
to hit on Tobago's Public Beach.

This was a folly wished on the island by the government in Port
of Spain. Tobago was girdled by wonderful beaches open to everyone, and would have preferred the money to be spent on something
useful, such as road-repairs. So nobody went to the Public Beach,
and Mr Burnett, who ran it, had such a boring time that he couldn't
wait to invite me to join him and his assistant for a drink on the

verandah of his little office. I told him my worry about the big hotel, and said: 'Surely there must be a hotel somewhere on the island where ordinary people stay?' There was a tiny pause while the two men avoided exchanging glances and I remembered with dismay that when people here said 'ordinary' they meant 'black' in a rude way; then Mr Burnett kindly chose to take the word as I had intended it, and said of course there was: his old friend Mr Louis was opening one that very week, and he would take me there at once.

So I became – it seemed like a dream, such a delightful happening coming so pat – Mr Louis's first guest in the Hotel Jan de Moor: a former estate house in pretty grounds, scrupulously run and not expensive. Mr Louis had reckoned that American tourists would soon include American black people – school teachers and so on – who would expect comfort but would be unable to pay silly prices, so he had decided to cater for the likes of them. In that first week the only people who visited were his neighbours, dropping in for a drink in the bar as dusk fell, which made it almost as friendly as staying in a private house, and I have never enjoyed a hotel more.

That whole holiday was a joy, not only because it was my introduction to the beauties of tropical seas, shores and forests, but because I *knew the place so well*. Of course I had always been aware of how well V. S. Naipaul and Michael Anthony wrote, but until I had stepped off an aeroplane into the world they were writing about I had not quite understood what good writing can do. There were many moments, walking down a street in Port of Spain, or driving a bumpy road between walls of sugar cane or under coconut palms, when I experienced an uncanny twinge of *coming home*; which made the whole thing greatly more interesting and moving than even the finest ordinary sightseeing can be. And after that I was always to find what I think of as the anti-Mustique side of the Caribbean, dreadful though its problems can be, amazingly congenial.

In the nineteen-seventies we went through an odd, and eventually comic, experience: to the outward eye we were taken over by Time/Life. 'Synergy' had suddenly become very much the thing among giant corporations, and on one of his New York trips André had allowed himself to be persuaded that we would benefit greatly if he sold a considerable chunk of shares in André Deutsch Limited to that company. Piers and I both think it must have been about forty per cent, but we were never told. The chief – indeed, the only – argument in favour of doing so was that already the advances being paid for important books were beginning to sky-rocket beyond our reach, and with Time/Life as our partners we could keep up with that trend.

I was present at the London meeting where the beauties of the scheme were explained to our board by two or three beaming Time/Lifers who appeared to be describing some mysterious charity founded for the benefit of small publishers. At one point I asked a question which was genuinely puzzling me: 'But what do you see as being in it for *you*?' After a fractional pause, a gentle blast of pure waffle submerged the question, and I was left believing what in fact I continued to believe: *that they didn't know*. Shrewd predatory calculations *might* be underlying all this, but it seemed unlikely. 'Can it be,' I asked André after the meeting, 'that they are just silly?' To which he answered crisply: 'Yes.' I think he had already started to wonder what on earth he was doing, but couldn't see how to back out of it.

Oh well, we all thought, perhaps we *will* get some big books through them, and they don't seem to intend any harm – and the truth was, they did not. We got one big book through them – Khrushchev's memoirs in two volumes, the first of which was sniffed at suspiciously by reviewers who thought it was written by the CIA, and the second of which was claimed by Time/Life to be proved genuine by scientific means, but who cared? They made no attempt to intervene in any of our publishing plans. And they drove André mad.

This they did by writing to him from time to time, asking him for a detailed forecast of our publishing plans for the next five years. The first time they did this he sent a civil reply explaining that our kind of publishing didn't work like that, but gradually he became more and more enraged. I remember being taken aside at a New York party by the man who functioned as our link with Time/Life, and asked to calm André and explain to him that all he need do to keep the accounts people happy was *send a few figures*. He didn't say in so many words 'It doesn't matter if they make sense or not', but he very clearly implied as much, and that was the message I carried home . . . which made André even madder. It was their silliness that was getting to him, not their asking for information. Our accountant Philip Tammer (who, by the way, was the dearest, kindest, most long-suffering, most upright and most loyal accountant anyone ever had) once wrote to their accountants: 'What we will be publishing in five years' time depends on what's going on in the head of some unknown person probably sitting in a garret, and we don't know the address of that garret.' André was feeling about Time/Life very much what I felt about André when he nagged the editorial department about lack of method.

The other cause of indignation was the Annual Meeting of the Associates (there were ten or so other companies linked to

Time/Life, like us). Sales conferences in exotic venues were much
indulged in during the seventies – perhaps they still are? They were
justified on the grounds that giving the reps a treat would improve
their morale. This was not a belief subscribed to by anyone in our
firm. On one occasion we ventured as far as a pub outside
Richmond, but usually at the end of the conference we all sloped
off to dinner at an inexpensive restaurant, the meal (if André had
managed to get his oar in) ordered in advance so that no one could
start getting silly with the smoked salmon (and they were fun,
those evenings). So the idea of traipsing off to *Mexico* for what
amounted to a glorified sales conference, as he had to do in the first
year of this alliance, seemed to André an outrage. For the second
year they announced that the venue would be Morocco, and he
struck. He wrote to them severely, pointing out that all the
Associates would be going, like him, to the Frankfurt Book Fair, so
the obvious time and place for their meeting would be the weekend
before the Fair, somewhere in Germany within easy reach of
Frankfurt. I distinctly heard the sound of gritted teeth behind the
fulsome letter received in return, which assured him that 'this is
exactly the kind of input we were hoping to gain from our
Associates'.

Before each meeting all the Associates were asked to think up ten
Publishing Projects (which meant books), and to send their out-
lines to New York, where they would be pooled, printed, and bound
in rich leather, one copy each for every delegate with his name
impressed on it in gold, to await him on the conference table.
'Thinking up' books on demand is one of the idlest occupations in
all of publishing. If an interesting book has its origins in a head
other than its author's, then it either comes in a flash as a result of
compelling circumstances, or it is the result of someone's obsession

which he has nursed until just the right author has turned up. Books worth reading don't come from people saying to each other 'What a good idea!'. They come from someone knowing a great deal about something and having strong feelings about it. Which does not mean that a capable hack can't turn out a passable book-like object to a publisher's order; only that when he does so it ends on the remainder shelves in double-quick time.

So we asked each other 'Do you think that all the other Associates are feeling just like us?' – and what we were feeling was a blend of despair and ribaldry. We had a special file labelled 'Stinkers', kept in a bottom drawer of André's desk, which contained a collection of all the most appalling ideas that had been submitted to us over the years, and I dug this out . . . But finally sobriety prevailed and we settled for two or three notions so drab that I have forgotten them. No one else, André reported, did any better, so they *had* all been feeling like us.

Two years were as many as André could stand of Time/Life – and probably as much as they could stand of him. He never divulged which side it was who first said 'Let's call it a day', nor how much money was lost on the deal when he bought the shares back, but his delight at being free of them was manifest. I thought of pressing him for details, and so, I think, did Piers, but it would have been too unkind. The silliness had not all been on the other side.

Since starting this chapter about our long and mostly happy time in Great Russell Street I have spent hours remembering colleagues, remembering authors, remembering books . . . colleagues, especially. I suppose people who choose to work with books and are good at their jobs are not inevitably likeable, but they very often are; and if you see them every day over long periods of time, collaborating with them in various ways as you do so, they become more than likeable. They become a pleasing part of your life. Esther Whitby, Ilsa Yardley, Pamela Royds, Penny Buckland, June Bird, Piers Burnett, Geoff Sains, Philip Tammer . . . : I can't write about them in the sense of making them come alive and interesting to people who know nothing about them, without embarking on a different kind of book, and one which is, I fear, beyond my range, so I will just have to go on carrying them, and others, in my head for my own pleasure. And it's for my own satisfaction that I now say how glad I am to have them there.

The authors: well, about a few of them I shall write in Part Two. And the books: there were too many of them, and anyway nothing is more boring than brief descriptions of books which one has not read. But two of them have floated to the surface as being of great value to me. Neither of them was part of a literary career; neither of them sold well; neither of them will be remembered by many readers. What is remarkable about both of them is the person who speaks.

Over and over again one sees lives which appear to have been shaped almost entirely by circumstances: by a cruel childhood, perhaps, or (like Franz Stangl's) by a corrupt society. These two stories are told by a man and a woman who, if shaping by circumstances were an immutable law, would have been hopeless wrecks. They did not just survive what would have finished off a great many people: they survived it triumphantly.

The first of these books is *Parents Unknown: A Ukrainian Childhood*, by Morris Stock. He was found as a newborn baby on the steps of a synagogue in a small Ukrainian town; was shunted around the Jewish community to various foster parents, ending with a brutal couple who almost killed him. If an interfering peasant woman hadn't made a fuss when she noticed a little boy almost dead with cold, waiting on a wagon outside an inn, they would quite have done so. The community stepped in again, and he was passed on to a grain-merchant who was eventually to work him very hard, but who treated him well. Almost at once he began to be liked and trusted, learning how to read and write and mastering his trade: it seems that as soon as he was free to be himself he revealed intelligence, resilience and generosity. Before he was twenty he had set up business on his own, married a girl he was to love for the rest of her life, and decided to move to London, where he spent the next fifty years prospering, and raising a family remarkable for talent and ability. He was an old man when his daughter persuaded him to write his story, which he did with vigour and precision – a very charming old man. Some quality at the centre of Morris Stock had been able to triumph over formidable odds.

And the same was true of Daphne Anderson, who wrote *The Toe-Rags*. By the time I met her Daphne was the beautiful wife of a retired general, living in Norfolk, better-read and more amusing in a gentle way than I expected a general's wife to be. It was astounding to learn that this woman had once been a barefoot, scabby-legged little girl whose only dress was made from a sugar-sack, knowing nothing beyond the Rhodesian bush and speaking an African language – Shona – better than she spoke English. Her parents were the poorest of poor whites, victims of her father's uselessness: he was stupid, bad-tempered, utterly self-centred, incompetent and irresponsible. He dumped her wretched mother, with three children, in the bush and left them there for months on end, sending no money. She scraped by, by allowing occasional favours to such men as were about, and the children were looked after by Jim, their Shona servant (no white could be so poor as not to have a servant: it was like Charles Dickens's family taking their little maid into debtors' prison with them). Jim saved not only Daphne's life, but also her spirit, being a rock of kindness and good sense for the children to cling to.

Not surprisingly, when a decent man asked the mother to go off with him she did, taking her new baby but leaving the three other children in the belief that their father would be arriving next day. She thought that if no one else was there he would *have* to cope. He did not turn up. Three days later Jim, having run out of food, walked them to the nearest police station. They never saw their mother again, and had the misfortune to be delivered into the hands of their father's sister. She was like him in every way except in being (although unable to read) ruthlessly competent, so that she had become rich by running a brick kiln. She took the children in because of 'What would the neighbours say?', then took it out on them by consigning them to the kitchen: where, once again, they were saved by an African man – her cook. He provided kindness, common sense about good behaviour, and a comforting sense of irony. Their aunt it was who dubbed them the Toe-Rags.

There followed, until Daphne was in her twenties, a long chain of deprivation and disturbing events, with one blessing in their midst: Daphne was sent to a convent school. Right from the beginning the child had fallen on every tiny scrap of good that came her way – every kindness, every chance to learn, every opportunity to discriminate between coarse and fine, stupid and wise, ugly and beautiful, mean and generous. School came to her – in spite of agonizing embarrassment over unpaid bills and having no clothes – as a feast of pleasure. She does not, of course, tell her story as that of an astonishing person. She tells it for what happened, and out of delighted amazement at her own good luck. It is the reader who sees that this person who should have been a wreck had somewhere within her a centre so strong that all she needed were the smallest openings in order to be good and happy.

I loved that book even more than I loved Morris Stock's; and both of them I loved not for being well-written (though both were written well enough for their purposes), but because of what those two people were like. They brought home to me the central reason why books have meant so much to me. It is not because of my pleasure in the art of writing, though that has been very great. It is because they have taken me so far beyond the narrow limits of my own experience and have so greatly enlarged my sense of the complexity of life: of its consuming darkness, and also – thank God – of the light which continues to struggle through.

11

Although André's chief instrument for office management was always, from 1946 to 1984, the threatening of Doom, he was slow to recognize its actual coming. For a long time he preferred to interpret its symptoms as temporary blips.

The demise of our house, a slow process, was caused by a combination of two things: the diminishing number of people who wanted to read the kind of book we mostly published, and the recession.

Ever since we started in business books had been becoming steadily more expensive to produce: the eight and sixpenny novel became the ten and sixpenny novel, then the twelve and sixpenny, then the fifteen shilling (that seemed a particularly alarming jump) – after which the crossing of the hitherto unthinkable one pound barrier came swiftly. (What would we have thought if some Cassandra had told us that soon eight, ten, twelve, fifteen, twenty would be enumerating pounds, not shillings?) After each rise people continued to buy books – though not quite so many people.

André was impatient of the idea that the falling-off was caused by anything other than the rise in price . . . But *everything* was costing more – that was life, people were used to it: it seemed to me that something else was at work. Which was proved true by several attempts, made by ourselves and others, to bring out cheap editions of first novels of a kind categorized as 'literary': making them cheaper did not make them sell better.

People who buy books, not counting useful how-to-do-it books, are of two kinds. There are those who buy because they love books and what they can get from them, and those to whom books are one form of entertainment among several. The first group, which is by far the smaller, will go on reading, if not for ever, then for as long as one can foresee. The second group has to be courted. It is the second which makes the best-seller, impelled thereto by the buzz that a particular book is really something special; and it also makes publishers' headaches, because it has become more and more resistant to courting.

The Booker Prize was instigated in 1969 with the second group in mind: make the quality of a book *news* by awarding it an impressive amount of *money*, and *hoi polloi* will prick up their ears. It worked in relation to the books named; but it had been hoped that after buying the winner and/or the runners-up, people would be 'converted' to books in general, and there was no sign of that. Another attempt to stir the wider public's consciousness resulted in the slogan 'Books are Best' which still chirps its message from booksellers' carrier bags – and is surely the kind of advertising that is not even *seen* by those who do not want the advertised object.

What has been happening is that slowly – very slowly, so that often the movement was imperceptible – group number two has been floating away into another world. Whole generations have grown up to find images more entertaining than words, and the roaming of space via a computer more exciting than turning a page. Of course a lot of them still read; but progressively a smaller lot, and fewer and fewer can be bothered to dig into a book that offers any resistance. Although these people may seem stupid to us, they are no stupider than we are: they just enjoy different things. And although publishers like André Deutsch Limited went on having a happy relationship with group number one, and still, throughout the seventies, hit it off quite often with group number two, the distance between what the publisher thought interesting and what the wider public thought interesting was widening all the time.

Surely, I used to think as we moved into the eighties, we ought to be able to do something about this? Look at Allen Lane, in the thirties, thinking up Penguin Books: that had been a revolution in publishing to meet a need . . . couldn't we do something like it in a different way? Piers and I discussed it occasionally (André couldn't be bothered with such idle speculation), but we never got anywhere. Piers thought we should cut down on fiction and look for serious non-fiction of a necessary kind, and he was right; but it was easier said than done. I just went blank. I was too stuck in my ways to want to change, that was my trouble. We had been publishing books we liked for so long that the thought of publishing any other kind was horrible. So let's talk about something else . . . Which must have been more or less what André was feeling under his irritability.

Meanwhile recession was approaching. The first time it sent a shiver down my spine was when Edward Heath ordained a three-day week. Down we go, I thought, and how could anyone expect anything else when a country which was once the centre of a vast empire had become a little island off the shores of Europe? Gone are the days when we could buy cheap and sell dear – other people are going to pinch our markets . . . Perhaps this crisis will pass, but it would be foolish to suppose that it is going, in any permanent way, *to get better*.

The feeling was so similar to those moments before the Second World War when one suddenly saw that it was going to happen, that all I could do was react as I had reacted then: shut my eyes tight and think of something else. André, after all, said that I was exaggerating, and he was much better at economic matters than I was . . . I managed to avert my mind from the depressing prospect so successfully that the rest of the seventies and the early eighties passed quite cheerfully; but I was not in the least surprised when recession was declared.

André talked very little about selling the firm. I knew, quite early in the eighties, that he was half-heartedly sniffing around for an offer, and he had stated his reason as clearly as he would ever do: 'It's not any fun any more,' is what he said.

And it was not. He could no longer make those exciting swoops on 'big' books because the firms which had combined into conglomerates could always outbid us; and the 'literary' books at which we had been good . . . well, I was beginning to hope, when a typescript arrived on my desk, that it would be bad. If it was bad, out it went and no hassle. If it was good – then ahead loomed the editorial conference at which we would have to ask ourselves 'How many do you reckon it will sell?', and the honest answer would probably be 'About eight hundred copies'. Whereupon we would either have to turn down something good, which was painful, or else fool ourselves into publishing something that lost money. We still brought out some good things – quite a number of them – during those years, and by careful cheese-paring André kept the firm profitable (just) until at last he did sell it; but there are some embarrassing books on our eighties lists: obvious (though never, I am glad to say, shameful) attempts to hit on something 'commercial' which only proved that we were not much good at it. And André was already starting to fall asleep during editorial conferences.

He never surprised me more than when he announced, on returning from the annual book-trade jamboree in the United States, that he had found the right person to buy the firm.

'Who?'

'Tom Rosenthal.'

'Are you mad?'

This reaction was not dictated by my own feelings: I had glimpsed Tom only occasionally at parties. It was because André had always seemed to dislike him. Tom began his career in 1959 with Thames and Hudson, which specialized in art books, and why he left them in 1970 I don't know. Probably it was because he felt drawn to a more literary kind of publishing, since his next job, starting in 1971, was managing director of Secker & Warburg, and in the short interval between the two he had played with the idea of launching his own list, and had visited André to discuss the possibility of doing it under our wing. It was then that André had been rude – not to him, but about him. It seemed to be simply the dissimilarity of their natures that put him off.

André was small and dapper; Tom was large, with the slightly rumpled look of many bearded men, though he was far from being among the seriously shaggy. André was a precise and dashing driver; Tom was too careless and clumsy to trust himself to drive at all. André, without being prissy, was nearer to being fastidious in his speech than he was to being coarse; Tom evidently liked to shock. And above all, André abhorred extravagance, while Tom enjoyed it. They were also very different in their pleasures. André had no important pleasures outside his work except for going to the theatre (he never missed a well-reviewed West End play, and adventured into the fringe quite often), and skiing, which he adored; Tom took no exercise except for a daily swim for his health (his back had been badly damaged in a traffic accident), preferred opera to plays, gave much time and thought to his collection of first editions, and had also built up an impressive collection of paintings – many of which André thought were ugly. They were not designed to be friends.

But now André *needed* someone to buy the firm, so when Tom, who had become a director of the Heinemann group in 1972, told him that he was fed up with administration and longed to get back into hands-on book producing, he suddenly saw that he had been wrong about this brilliant publisher who was a much nicer man than anyone realized, and who – best of all – was our kind of person, so would not want to turn our firm into something else . . . As it would turn out, that 'best of all' summed up precisely why Tom was the *wrong* man, but the fact escaped us all: I can't think why, given that most of us were well aware that the firm needed to change.

The negotiations, which took place under the guidance of Arnold (Lord) Goodman, the ubiquitous fixer and smoother, lasted a long time. André never told anyone how much Tom paid for the firm, but we all knew that he was to pay in two stages. On putting down the first half of the money he would come in as joint managing director with André, and two years later (or perhaps it was three), when he put down the rest, he would become the sole managing director and André would be awarded the title of President and continue to have a room in the office if he wanted it, but would cease to have any say in its affairs. I remember André telling me: 'Last week Arnold said I must remember that now the agreement has been signed the firm is *no longer mine*. He must think I'm dotty – of course I know that.'

But alas, alas! Of course he didn't.

Tom made the sensible suggestion that they should divide our authors between them and each be responsible for his own group without interfering in the other's. André agreed, but he was unable to keep to it. Over and over again he would pick up the intercom, or (worse) amble into Tom's room, to say something on the lines of 'If you are thinking of selling the German rights of such and such a book to Fischer Verlag, would you like me to drop a line to so-and-so?'. To start with Tom was civil: 'That's very kind, but I've done it already.' But he is a man with a short fuse and it was not long before he was snapping . . . and not long again before he was yelling. Whereupon André would come into my room and report querulously 'Tom *yelled* at me!'. And when I had extracted the details of the incident, and told him that it was his own fault for sticking his nose in when he knew how much it maddened Tom, in an even more querulous, almost tearful voice: 'But I was only trying to *help*!'

'Well, for God's sake *stop* trying to help. You know it doesn't do any good . . . and he doesn't do it to you.' And a few days later it would happen all over again.

Then André's pain began to turn into anger. He began to see almost everything that Tom did as wrong, and to complain endlessly – first to me, then to those other people in the office who were concerned with whatever he was complaining about, then to everyone in the office, putting out feelers for Tom's sins in the accounts department, the production department, even to the switchboard. Nearly everyone in the place was fond of André, and felt for him now that he was losing the firm that had so obviously meant so much to him for so long; but people began to be embarrassed by his behaviour and to lose sympathy with him. Burly, bluff, bearded Tom was not a man of delicate sensibility (was even inclined to boast of that fact, as he boasted about many things), and he *was* extravagant, so people had reservations about him; but they didn't feel he deserved this campaign against him. In fact, for quite a while after his arrival he cheered us up. If someone says loudly 'Though I say it myself, I'm a bloody good businessman', you tend to believe him simply because you can't believe anyone would be so crass as to say that, if he wasn't. Or at least I tended to believe it, and I think others did too. Tom liked to think big and generously, so if you said, for instance, that a book would be better with sixteen pages of illustrations – or even thirty-two – instead of the eight pages which André would have grudgingly allowed if he absolutely had to, Tom would say 'My dear girl, let it have as many as it *needs*', and that sort of response was invigorating. He brought in some interesting books, too – notably the first volume of David Cairns's magnificent biography of Berlioz – and a few big names including Elias Canetti and Gore Vidal; so for a year or so it was possible to believe that, given his flair as a businessman, he was going to revitalize the firm. You did not have to be particularly drawn to him to be pleased about that – or to be shocked when André began to extend his campaign outside the office. For some time I hoped it was only old friends to whom he was confiding his grievances, but gradually it became clear that he was going on and on and on to *everyone he met.*

And then came a substantial feature article in the *Independent* about the situation, telling the story entirely from André's point of view, with all its distortions, and making Tom look silly as well as disagreeable. Even the illustrations were slanted: André looking young and handsome, Tom, in a really unforgivable photograph, looking grotesque. Tom was convinced that the story must have come from interviews with André, and no one could deny that it did represent his opinions and emotions with remarkable fidelity. I have never been able to blame Tom for his fury. It was some time since they had spoken to each other. Now Tom forbade André to set foot in the office ever again, and be damned to the agreement about his continuing to have a room there. What else could he have done?

I have been reminded that I wrote funny letters to friends about all this – indeed, that one friend kept them for their funniness. But in retrospect it was far from funny. It became evident quite soon after André had been thrown out that his health had begun a long process of deterioration, and I now think this had started several years earlier, even before he sold the firm, when we first noticed him falling asleep during editorial conferences. He had always cried wolf about his health (you could safely bet that if you were just about to tell him that you were going down with 'flu, he would nip in ahead of you with angina pains), so I had a long-established habit of disregarding his complaints . . . But this time he would have denied that anything was wrong with him, so even if all of us had recognized that his ugly but pathetic campaign against the man he himself had chosen was not waged by a well man, we could have done nothing about it.

My shares in André Deutsch Limited were so few that I made very

little money from the sale of the company, and I had hardly any
other income, so I was grateful when Tom told me that if I were
willing to stay on at the salary I was earning when he took over, he
would be glad to have me for as long as I could keep going. I was
seventy by then, and would not start feeling like an old woman till
I turned eighty; but in spite of that comparative spryness, having
never been a specially good copy-editor (picker-up of spelling mistakes and so on), I was now a bad one, and often alarmed myself
when I read something a second time and saw how many things I
had missed on the first run-through. I was therefore less valuable
than I should have been at that side of the job; and in its larger
aspects . . . well, I was still sure that I could tell good writing from
bad, but was I able to judge what people the age of my grandchil-
dren, if I'd had them, would want to buy? No – no more able than
Tom was. We often liked the same books, among them Pete Davies's
The Last Election, Boman Desai's *The Memory of Elephants*, David
Gurr's *The Ring Master*, Llorenç Villalonga's *The Doll's Room*, Chris
Wilson's *Blueglass* – each in its own way, I am still prepared to
swear, very good: but none of them money-makers. So I could
make no contribution in that way. Friends said 'He's getting you
cheap', but I didn't think he was. I thought I was lucky in still earning money, and that although the job was 'not any fun any more', it
could have been much worse.

But quite soon three depressing things happened: Tom sold the
whole of the André Deutsch Limited archive; he sold the children's
books; and he got rid of warehousing and sales, handing all that
side of the publishing operation over to Gollancz.

It was sentimentality to feel the loss of that intractable mountain
of old files so keenly – we had kept copies of essential matter such
as contracts, and never suffered in any practical way from the

absence of the rest; but it did, all the same, give me a most uncomfortable feeling. A publishing house without its archive – there was something shoddy about it, like a bungalow without a damp course. And where was the money which came in as a result? – a question even more obtrusive when it came to the sale of the children's books, for which he got a million pounds. We all supposed, in the end, that Tom must have had to borrow heavily in order to buy us, and was now selling off bits of us in order to pay off his debt – which, naturally, he had a perfect right to do; he would have had the right to spend the money on prostitutes and polo ponies, if he liked. But he had given us the impression that he had sold the children's books in order to get the firm back onto an even keel, and that was only too evidently not happening. Fortunately Pamela Royds and the list which she had built up single-handed with so much loving care and unremitting labour (the most profitable thing under our roof, into the bargain!) were well-served by the change. Scholastic Press, which bought them, was a prosperous firm specializing in children's books, which had a first-rate sales organization, and Pam reported that it was delicious to breathe such invigorating air after the oppressive atmosphere of the last few years at Deutsch. While for us . . . It was like having a hand chopped off with a promise that it would result in a magic strengthening of the rest of the body, and then finding oneself as wobbly as ever and minus a hand into the bargain.

While as for losing control of one's sales organization . . . Surely Tom must know that however good the intentions, no one ever ran someone else's sales as well as they ran their own? Surely he must know that this move is the beginning of the end? When asked what the situation was, all he would ever answer was 'It would be fine if it weren't for *the bloody bank*'. From which we all concluded that they had over-indulged the firm hideously with a gigantic over-draft, which now he had somehow got to pay off, or else!

And indeed, there was soon a man from the bank sitting in on meetings, and any number of little chisellings going on: people who left not being replaced, books postponed because printers couldn't be paid, lies being told for fear of loss of face . . . It is depressing to remember that time, and pointless to describe it in detail. What it boiled down to was that Tom's claim to be a bloody good businessman was poppycock, because no businessman who was any good would have bought our firm at that time, and then imagined that he could go on running it as the same kind of firm only more so. It was a fantasy, and he was lucky to get clear of it in the end, having at last found someone willing to buy the firm for, I suppose, the name and the building. To a man unable easily to admit, or even discuss, failure, the experience must have been excruciating.

While those two last years were going on I did not allow myself to know how much I was hating them. I was frightened by the thought of living without my salary, and had become hypnotized, like a chicken with its beak pressed to a chalk line, by the notion of continuing to work for as long as possible. And when some quite minor incident jerked my beak off the line, and I thought 'This is absurd – I don't have to go on with this', elation was mixed with further alarm. I did not expect to be one of those people who find themselves at a complete loss when they retire – I would have a companion, a place that I loved, things to do – but my days had been structured by a job for all my adult life, and it seemed possible that freedom, at first, would feel *very odd*. I even had one fit of 3 a.m. angst, thinking 'This is like standing on the edge of a cliff with a cold wind blowing up my skirt!'.

But I was overlooking the extent to which I had been drained and depressed by trying not to admit how miserable I was, and as it turned out there was no cold wind at all. When I woke up to my first morning as a retired person, what I thought *at once* was 'I am happy!'. Happy, and feeling ten years younger. Instead of being sad that my publishing days were over, it was 'Thank God, thank God that I'm out of it at last'. And then, gradually, it became even better, because the further I move from the date of my retirement, the less important those last sad years in the office become, and the luckier I know myself to be in having lived all the years that went before them.

PART TWO

IN 1962 I WROTE – and meant – the following description of the relationship between publisher and writer.

It is an easy one, because the publisher usually meets his writers only after having read something they have written, and if he has thought it good it does not much matter to him what the man will be like who is about to come through his door. He is feeling well-disposed for having liked the work; the writer is feeling well-disposed for his work having been liked; neither is under obligation to attempt a close personal relationship beyond that. It is a warm and at the same time undemanding beginning, in which, if genuine liking is going to flower, it can do so freely.

That is true, but only as far as it goes. I find it surprising – perhaps even touching – that after sixteen years in the trade I was still leaving it at that, because although the beginning is, indeed, nearly always easy, the relationship as a whole is quite often not. I would now say that a friendship, properly speaking, between a publisher and a writer is . . . well, not impossible, but rare.

The person with whom the writer wants to be in touch is his reader: if he could speak to him directly, without a middleman, that is what he would do. The publisher exists only because turning someone's written words into a book (or rather, into several thousand books) is a complicated and expensive undertaking, and so is distributing the books, once made, to booksellers and libraries. From the writer's viewpoint, what a mortifying necessity this is: that the thing which is probably more important to him than anything else – the thing which he has spun out of his own guts over many months, sometimes with much pain and anxiety – should be denied its life unless he can find a middleman to give it physical existence, and will then agree that this person shall share whatever the book earns. No doubt all writers know in their heads that their publishers, having invested much money and work in their books, deserve to make a reasonable profit; but I am sure that nearly all of them feel in their hearts that whatever their books earn *ought* to belong to them alone.

The relationship is therefore less easy than I once supposed. Taking only those cases in which the publisher believes he has found a truly good writer, and is able to get real pleasure from his books, this is how it will go. The publisher will feel admiration for this man or woman, interest in his or her nature, concern for his or her welfare: all the makings of friendship. It is probably no exaggeration to say that he would feel honoured to be granted that person's friendship in return, because admiration for someone's work can excite strong feelings. But even so, part of the publisher's concern will be that of someone who has invested in a piece of property – how big a part depending on what kind of person the publisher is. With some people it would preponderate; with me, because of how useless I am as a business woman, it was very small indeed, but it was never non-existent. So there is potential complication, even looking at only one side of the relationship; and looking at the other side there is a great deal more.

In the writer the liking inspired by the publisher's enthusiasm may well be warm, but it will continue only if he thinks the publisher is doing a good job by making the book look pleasing and selling enough copies of it; and what the writer means by 'enough' is not always what the publisher means. Even if the publisher is doing remarkably well, he is still thinking of the book as one among many, and in terms of his experience of the market; while the writer is thinking in terms of the only book that matters in the world.

Of course writers' attitudes vary. I have known a few who, behind a thin veneer of civility, see their publisher in the way a man may see his tailor: a pleasant enough person while he is doing a good job, allowed a certain intimacy in that he has to know things the equivalent of your inner-leg measurement and whether you 'dress' to the left or the right – but you wouldn't ask him to dinner (such a writer is easy to work with but you don't like him). I have known others whose dependence on their publisher is as clinging as that of a juvenile tennis star on her parent (very boring). But generally the writer likes to like his publisher, and will go on doing so for years if he can; but will feel only mildly sorry if the publisher's poor performance, or what he sees as such, causes him to end the relationship. When the ending of a relationship causes no serious personal disturbance it cannot be called a friendship. The only André Deutsch authors whom I count among my real friends opened the way to that friendship by going off to be published by someone else.

But this is not to say that I haven't been *more interested* in some of 'my' authors than I have been in anyone else: haven't watched them more closely, speculated about them more searchingly, wondered at them with more delight – or dismay. Only two of them have actually played a part in my life (I have written books about both of them, *After a Funeral* and *Make Believe*). But several of them have enlarged my life; have been experiences in it in the way, I suppose, that a mountain is an experience to a climber, or a river to an angler; and the second part of this book is about six of those remarkable people.

MORDECAI RICHLER AND BRIAN MOORE

A FEW DAYS AGO I read *The Acrobats* again: Mordecai Richler's first novel which we published in 1954. I had not looked at it for forty-five years. 'Talk about a young man's book!' I said to myself. 'What on earth made us take it on?' It really is very bad; but something of its author's nature struggles through the clumsiness, and we were in the process of building a list, desperate for new and promising young writers. I must say that I congratulate André and myself for discerning that underpinning of seriousness and honesty (there was no hint of his wit), and think we deserved the reward of his turning out to be the writer he is.

Mordecai in himself presented rather the same kind of puzzle, in those days. I liked him very much from the moment of meeting him, but sometimes found myself asking 'Why?', because he hardly ever spoke: I have never known anyone else so utterly unequipped with small-talk as he was then. How could one tell that someone was generous, kind, honest and capable of being very funny if he hardly ever said a word? I still don't know how, but it happened: I was always sure that he was all those things, and soon understood that his not saying anything unless he had something to say was part of what made me so fond of him. He was the least phoney person imaginable, and still is today (though he has become much better at talking).

He and Brian Moore, to whom he introduced me, were the writers I had in mind when I wrote the optimistic paragraph quoted five pages back. I was thirty-seven by then, but the war had acted on time rather as brackets act on a text: when one got back to normal life it felt in some ways like a continuation of what had preceded the interruption, so even if you carried wartime scars you were suddenly younger than your actual years. When those two men were new on our list and in my life, the days had a flavour of discovery, amusement and pleasure which now seems odd in the light of chronology, but was very agreeable. By then, of course, I had already met a number of writers whom I admired, but those two were the first good writers I thought of as friends; and also (although I didn't notice this at the time) the first two men I had ever deeply liked without any sex in the relationship. Our relationship depended on their writing – something which mattered to each of them more than anything else, and which happened to interest me more than anything else: that was what created the warmth and made the absence of sexual attraction irrelevant.

Although I felt more attached to Mordecai than to Brian, I got to know Brian better – or so I thought. This was partly because I was more aware of being older than Mordecai, partly because of Mordecai's taciturnity, and partly because of his women. His first wife combined a good deal of tiresomeness with many endearing qualities, so that impatience with her was inevitably accompanied by guilt – an uncomfortable state, so that I sought their company less often than I might have done. And Florence, his second wife, was so beautiful that she used to daunt me. I am happy to say that I have become able to see through Florence's beauty (which endures) to all the other reasons why she remains the best-loved woman of my acquaintance; but in the past Mordecai did rather disappear into his marriage with this lovely person (you only have to read *Barney's Version* – the latest, and to my mind best, of his novels – to see that Mordecai knows all about *coups de foudre*). Added to which they went back to Canada: a distancing which certainly made it easier to accept his leaving us without bitterness.

And before he left I had the delight of seeing him come into his own. Both his second and third novels had been better than his first, but both were still dimmed by a youthful earnestness, so *The Apprenticeship of Duddy Kravitz*, in which he broke through to the wit and ribaldry that released his seriousness into the atmosphere, so to speak, was a triumph. If it had come after his leaving us, I would have been sad; instead, I was able to be proud. And the last of his books with us (until, much later, he invaded our children's list), *The Incomparable Atuk*, although it wilted a little towards its end, was for most of its length so funny that it still makes me laugh aloud. So he left pleasure behind him. And – this was the most important specific against bitterness – I understood exactly why he went, and would even have thought him daft if he had not done so. Mordecai was living by his pen; he had a growing family to support; and someone else was prepared to pay him more money than we did. A great advantage of not being a proper publisher with all a proper publisher's possessive territorial instincts is that what you mind about most is that good books should get published.

Naturally you would like the publisher to be yourself, but it is not the end of the world if it is someone else.

It was Mordecai who introduced me to Brian Moore in that he told me that this friend of his had written an exceptionally good book which we ought to go after; but I must not deprive André of his discovery of *Judith Hearne*. As André remembers it, he was given the book by Brian's agent in New York on the last day of one of his – André's – visits there; he read it on the plane on the way home and decided at once that he must publish it. I think it likely that he *asked* to see it, having been alerted, as I had been, by Mordecai. But whether or not he asked for it, he certainly recognized its quality at once; and when he handed it over to me, it came to me as something I was already hoping to read, and its excellence was doubly pleasing because Brian was a friend of Mordecai's. The two had got to know each other in Paris, and in Canada, where Mordecai was a native and Brian, an Ulsterman, had chosen to live in common – although the Moores moved to New York soon after we met.

Before Brian wrote *Judith Hearne* (later retitled *The Lonely Passion of Judith Hearne* for publication in paperback and in the United States), when he was scrabbling about to keep a roof over his head, he had written several thrillers for publication as pocketbooks, under a pseudonym, which he said had been a useful apprenticeship in story-telling because it was a law of the genre that something must happen on every page. But however useful, it came nowhere near explaining *Judith*. With his first serious book Brian was already in full possession of his technical accomplishment, his astounding ability to put himself into other people's shoes, and his particular view of life: a tragic view, but one that does not make a fuss about tragedy, accepting it as part of the fabric with which we all have to make do. He was to prove incapable of writing a bad book, and his considerable output was to include several more that were outstandingly good; but to my mind he never wrote anything more moving and more true than *Judith Hearne*.

When he came to London in 1955 for the publication of *Judith*, he came without his wife Jackie – perhaps she was in the process of moving them to New York. He was a slightly surprising figure, but instantly likeable: a small, fat, round-headed, sharp-nosed man resembling a robin, whose flat Ulster accent was the first of its kind I had heard. He was fat because he had an ulcer and the recommended treatment in those days was large quantities of milk; and also because Jackie was a wonderful cook. (Her ham, liberally injected with brandy before she baked it – she kept a medical syringe for the purpose – was to become one of my most poignant food memories.) When I asked him home to supper on that first visit he was careful to explain that he was devoted to his wife – a precaution which pleased me because it was sensible as well as slightly comic.

Few men would be considerate enough to establish their unavailability like that. (Perhaps I was flattering him: it may have been a touch of puritanical timidity that he was exhibiting, rather than considerateness. But that was how I saw it.) Once he was sure that I was harbouring no romantic or predatory fancies, the way was opened to a relaxed friendship, and for as long as I knew him and Jackie as a couple there seemed to be nothing that we couldn't talk about. They were both great gossips – and when I say great I mean great, because I am talking about gossip in its highest and purest form: a passionate interest, lit by humour but above malice, in human behaviour. We used often, of course, to talk about writing – his and other people's, and eventually mine – but much more often we would talk with glee, with awe, with amazement, with horror, with delight, about what people had done and why they had done it. And we munched up our own lives as greedily as we did everyone else's.

In addition to seeing the Moores when they came to England (once they rented a house in Chelsea which had a Francis Bacon hanging in the drawing-room) I spent half a holiday with them in Villefranche (the other half had been with the Richlers in Cagnes), crossed the Atlantic with them on board the *France*, stayed with them in New York and twice in their summer house in Amagansett. It was from Brian himself that I heard, in Villefranche, the story of how he came to move to Canada.

It was a painful and romantic story. Immediately after the war Brian had got a job in the relief force, UNRRA, which had taken him to Poland, and there he fell in love with a woman older than himself (or perhaps he had fallen already and went there in pursuit of her). It was a wild passion, undiminished by the fact that she was an alcoholic. The only effect of that misfortune was to make him drink far beyond his capacity in an attempt to keep up with her: he described with horror waking up on the floor of a hotel bedroom lying in his vomit, not knowing what day it was; crawling on his hands and knees to the bathroom for a drink of water; getting drunk again as the water stirred up the vodka still in him; and finally discovering that he had been unconscious for two whole days. And there had never been anything but flashes of happiness in the affair because he had never known where he was with her, whether because of the swerving moods of drunkenness, or because she despised the abjectness of his obsession, I am not sure. He remembered it as an agonizing time, but when she told him it was over and went away to Canada, although he tried to accept it, he couldn't. He followed her – and she refused even to see him. And thus, he said, he learnt to detest the very idea of romantic passion.

Thus, too, he made his break with his native Ulster, and became distanced from (he never broke with) his rather conventional Catholic family, which gave him the necessary perspective on a great deal of the material he was to use in his novels. Not that he began at once to write seriously. Among the ways he earned his living during those early days in Canada was proof-reading for a newspaper, during which he met Jackie, who was a journalist. Then came those useful pocketbook thrillers – which must have paid pretty well, because by the time he felt secure enough to settle down to writing what he wanted to write, Jackie was able to stop working. Their son Michael was about two when I first met them, and although the comfort the Moores lived in was modest, it *was* comfort.

They gave the impression of being an exceptionally compatible pair: as good an advertisement as one could hope to find for *liking* one's spouse as opposed to being mad about him/her. They got on well with each other's friends; they shared the same tastes in books, paintings, household objects, food and drink – and, of course, gossip. They laughed a lot together and they loved Michael together. They were delightful to be with. I remember trying to decide which of them I found the better company and settling for a dead heat: with Brian there was the extra pleasure of writing talk, in which he was simultaneously unpretentious and deeply serious; with Jackie the extra amusement of woman talk, in which she was exceptionally honest and funny. I used to look forward to our meetings with whole-hearted pleasure.

*

We were to publish five of Brian's books: *Judith Hearne* in '55, *The Feast of Lupercal* in '58, *The Luck of Ginger Coffey* in '60, *An Answer from Limbo* in '63 and *The Emperor of Ice Cream* in '66. Why, having made this good start with him, did we not go on to publish all his books?

Well, we might have lost him *anyway* because of the frugality of our advertising. Book promotion, before the ways of thinking and behaving bred by television became established, depended almost entirely on reviews, which we always got; and on advertising in newspapers. Interviews and public appearances were rare, and only for people who were news in themselves, as well as writers, like our Alain Bombard who crossed the Atlantic in a rubber dinghy to prove that shipwrecked sailors could live off the sea if they knew how. A novelist had to stab his wife, or something of that sort, to get attention on pages other than those devoted to books. So when a novelist felt that his publisher sold too few copies, what he complained about was always under-advertising.

Publishers, on the other hand, knew that the sort of advertisements that books – even quite successful ones – could pay for were almost useless. Inflate them to the point at which they really might shift copies, and they would then cost more than the extra copies sold could bring in. Two kinds of advertisement did make sense: descriptions of all your forthcoming books in the trade papers, to which booksellers and librarians turned for information; and conspicuous announcements in big-circulation broadsheets, devoted to a single book provided it was by an already famous author. The run-of-the-mill ad, a six or eight or ten inch column (sometimes double, more often single) into which as many books as possible had been squashed ... For my part, I only had to ask myself: when had I even looked at such an ad (except for one of our own, to check that nothing had gone wrong with it), to say nothing of buying something because of it? It was reviews, and people talking enthusiastically about books that made me buy them, and why should other people be different? Yet we went on running those pointless, or almost pointless, ads – as few of them as we could get away with – simply so that we could keep our authors happy by reporting 'Your book was advertised in newspapers A, B, C, D, E and F', hoping they would be enough impressed by this true statement not to ask 'And how many other books were in the same ad, and how big was the space, and where was it on the page?'. Often they were sufficiently impressed; but Brian quite soon began to be not impressed enough. By his third novel he had started to think that it ought to be treated like a novel by Graham Greene.

Given the quality of Brian's books, if we had indeed given them big solo ads in big-circulation newspapers, and done it often enough, we would no doubt have made him as famous as Greene. But a) it would have taken quite a long time to work, b) all our other writers would meanwhile be going into conniptions, and c) we could not afford it. Or so André was convinced. And in André Deutsch Limited no one but André Deutsch himself had a hope in hell of deciding how much money was to be spent on what. When André dismissed the idea of shifting the advertising of Brian's work into the big-time category as nonsense, all I could do – all, I must admit, I ever dreamt of doing – was convey his opinion to Brian in less brutal words. And up to the publication of *The Emperor of Ice Cream* in 1966 Brian did no more than mutter from time to time, and then appear to forget it.

Not long after that publication I went to New York for the firm, saw the Moores as usual, and was invited by them to spend a few days in Amagansett. The misery of New York in a heat-wave gives those easy-going Long Island seaside towns great charm: their tree-shaded streets, their shingled houses set back from the streets and far apart, among more trees – how pretty and restful they are! The English pride themselves on having evolved in the eighteenth century a perfect domestic architecture, but I think the Americans beat them at it with the unpretentious, graceful, welcoming wooden houses that are so respectfully and unpompously preserved in New England. The house rented by the Moores was not particularly distinguished, but the moment you were through the front door you were comfortable in it – and 'comfortable' was the word for Amagansett as a whole. It has (or had then) a life of its own apart from accommodating summer visitors, although that was what it chiefly did; and it wasn't smart. Its regular visitors insisted a little too much on how they preferred it to the snobby Hamptons, where the vast country retreats of the robber barons still stood, and where the big money still tended to go; but I thought Amagansett really did deserve preference. It was favoured by writers and medical people, particularly psychiatrists. When I arrived this time Brian and Jackie were full of a party ending with a moonlit swim, during which four or five drunk psychiatrists had been so relaxed and happy that, as they bobbed about in the sea, they had confided in each other their most intimate secrets: which were not, as ordinary people's might have been, what they did in bed, but *how much they earned*.

I was not the Moores' only guest. They had become friends with a couple whom I had met a year or so before, and liked: Franklin Russell, who wrote good and successful nature books, and his very attractive Canadian wife Jean, who was an actress – a good one according to the Moores, although she found it impossible to get parts in New York because Americans never took Canadians seriously. Frank was travelling in some inhospitable place for one of his books, so Jean needed cheering up and was therefore with us. The two couples had become so close that they had just pooled their resources and bought a country place in New Jersey: the Moores were going to live in the old farm house, the Russells were converting its barn. This venture was the summer's big excitement.

I was there for three or four days which were as enjoyable as our times together always were. On one of the days Jean took over the kitchen and cooked a supremely delicious shrimp dish, for which she was famous, and on another day she and Brian had to make the long drive to the new property, to sort something out with the builders, so Jackie and I made an outing to Sag Harbor. On my last day, as we were all strolling to the beach, Jackie and ten-year-old Michael leading the way, I caught myself thinking 'Perhaps darling Jackie is letting her indifference to appearance go a bit far'. Like Brian, she was fat, and she had recently become fatter – her ragged old denim shorts were too tight. And she had been neglecting her roughly blonded hair, which looked chopped rather than cut and was stiff from sea-bathing so that it stuck out like straw. When you couldn't see her vivid face and the brightness of her hazel eyes, you noticed that she was looking a mess. I don't recall making the comparison, but the always remarkable and apparently effortless physical elegance of Jean, who was walking beside me, may well have triggered the thought.

It was, however, a passing one: something which I would not have remembered if I had not received a letter from Jackie about a month later, telling me that Brian and Jean had run away together.

My first reaction was a shock of shame at my own obtuseness. Did

I not pride myself on being a shrewd observer of people's behaviour? How could I possibly have registered no more than that one tiny flicker of foreboding, and then dismissed it? So much for perceptiveness! And so much for Brian's detestation of romantic passion!

My next, and enduring, reaction was one of acute consternation on Jackie's behalf. She, too, had failed to pick up any hint of what was going on. She had made her discovery through some cliché of marital disaster such as finding a note in a pocket when sending a jacket to the cleaner. Trying not to be entirely sure of its implications, she had asked Brian for an explanation: out it all came, and off they went. She was still in shock when she wrote, and all my feelings of sympathy were for her and Michael.

It was only for a few days, however, that I felt Brian to have transmogrified into a villain. It did seem extraordinary that he and Jean had been prepared to continue with the property-sharing plan once they had fallen in love, abandoning it only on being discovered. That was what it looked like then, to both Jackie and me. Later it occurred to me that they might well have been less cold-blooded towards Frank and Jackie than they seemed: that they might not have realized how irresistible their passion had become until that day they spent together 'sorting things out with the builders', or even after that. But even while I was still being shocked by their ruthlessness, I knew that falling in love happens, and once it has happened it can't be undone. And I also acknowledged that I and their other friends must have been wrong in seeing the partnership between Brian and Jackie as cloudless. Little though he had shown it, he must have been finding it oppressive for some time. It is absurd for anyone to believe himself aware of the ins and outs of other people's relationships, so it was absurd to blame Brian for finding in Jean something which he needed, and which Jackie could not give. (That he had done so was true, and remained true for the rest of his life.)

So I expected soon to emerge from total dismay at the Moores' break-up, and to see Brian again as himself. But for the moment the person I couldn't stop thinking about was Jackie. *She* had not wanted anything from the marriage that it didn't give her: she had been as proud of Brian as a writer as she had been happy with him as a companion, and now all that was gone. Ahead of her stretched emptiness; above and below and within and without was the horrible miasma of the humiliation which comes from rejection. Then there was the anxiety of how to bring Michael through this debacle – and, for that matter, of how he and she were going to manage on their own . . . if ever anyone deserved sympathy, she did. Whereas Brian had seen what he wanted and had taken it, while remaining perfectly secure in the part of his own territory that was most important to him: his writing. No one need feel sorry for Brian. So it was Jackie I wanted to support, which meant writing to her often; whereas if I wrote to Brian, I wouldn't know what to say.

I ought, therefore, to have kept silent, but I did not. On getting a brief note giving me an address for him (whether this came from him or his agent I can't remember), I answered it almost as briefly, saying that although I was sure that we would soon be back on our old footing, for the present I was feeling for Jackie so strongly that I would prefer it if he and I confined ourselves to business matters.

How I regret not keeping his reply; because its strangeness is far from being communicable by description. I did not keep it because, having shown it to André, I wanted never to see it again.

It began disagreeably but rationally: there would be no business letters because there would be no further business. He had been displeased for some time by our failure to advertise his books properly, so now he was finding a new publisher. Upsetting, but sensible: if the letter had ended there we would have come back with some kind of undertaking to improve our performance, and if that had failed to mollify him André would have written him off as an example of the greed and folly of authors, and I would have known sadly that we had lost him through our own fault. But the letter did not end there. It went on for another page and a half, and what it said, in what appeared to be a fever of self-righteous spite against the woman he had dumped, was that I had sided with Jackie, and no one who had done that could remain his friend. The tone of that letter left André as shocked as it left me: so shocked that Brian's was the only departure from our list that he made no attempt to prevent.

Mordecai told me at the time that other friends of the Moores had been taken aback by this 'He who is not with me is against me' attitude, which made it seem all the more extraordinary. I had never encountered what I now know to be quite a common phenomenon: a person who has smashed a partnership trying to shift the whole blame for the break onto the one he or she has abandoned. It is natural, I suppose, to recoil from guilt – especially so, perhaps, in someone who was raised, as Brian was, to have a sharp sense of sin. But I still think that such a blind determination to have your omelette without breaking your eggs is ugly – and stupid, too – and this first example of it to come my way seemed impossible to believe. And it still seems nearly so. That Brian, with his wonderfully benign relish for human follies and failings, should have flumped into gross self-deception in this way . . . It seemed that I was losing him twice over, first as my friend (and that was very painful), then as himself. That letter could not have been written by the man I had thought Brian to be.

It often happens in old age that when one looks back on events which once seemed amazing, they now seem explicable and even commonplace: a depressing consequence of responses made blunt by the passing of time. Perhaps I should be grateful to Brian for having done something which still gives me a jab of genuine dismay.

Jackie is dead. For a time it looked as though the story, for her, had taken an astonishingly happy turn – and a comic one, into the bargain. She and Franklin Russell, left with the task of sorting out the shared-property plan, became closer friends than ever, had an affair – and ended up married. She was not a spiteful person. I never heard her say a word against Brian stronger than an expression of puzzlement. But she did evidently enjoy telling me, just once, that in fact Frank had been quite glad to get rid of Jean. I got the impression that she was comfortable with Frank in rather the same way that Brian had, to begin with, been comfortable with her when recovering from his passion for his drunken love. I stayed with them once in the New Jersey house (they had sold the barn), and saw them happy enough together to be dealing bravely with the first of the disasters which hit them: the fact that their son Alexander had been born with spina bifida. He had by then reached the end of a long chain of operations, and was an enchanting little boy who seemed to be as active and cheerful as any other child of his age; and the core of Jackie's emotional life had obviously become her pride in him, and her happiness at having got him through to this state.

Soon after that visit she went with Frank on one of his journeys – I think it was the first time they had felt that they could briefly leave Alexander in other hands. On that journey she fell ill, and when she got home the illness was diagnosed as cancer of the pancreas. She fought it gallantly and died cruelly.

Frank and I did not know each other well enough to keep in touch, but I did run into him by chance about two years after her death. He had looked after her at home until the end and had been terribly shaken by what he had been through. I know that Michael Moore came together with his father after his mother's death, but what has happened to Franklin and Alexander Russell I do not know.

Although Brian's departure from our list was more painful than any other, it has never prevented me from remembering the years when he was with us with pleasure; and it made a substantial and valuable contribution to many a subsequent gossip-fest. There was very much more gain than loss in having published him. And my regret at hardly ever seeing Mordecai since he made that sensible move in his career, though very real, is softened by being able to read his books and being proud that we were his first publisher. When I finished reading *Barney's Version* I felt nothing but delight at his having so triumphantly outlived his first publishing house; and I am happy to end this chapter remembering that I once said to him 'You are going to end up as a Grand Old Man of Canadian Literature'. That is exactly what he would have done, if it were possible for a Grand Old Man to be wholly without pomposity.

JEAN RHYS

No one who has read Jean Rhys's first four novels can suppose that she was good at life; but no one who never met her could know how very bad at it she was. I was introduced to the novels quite early in the fifties, by Francis Wyndham, who was one of their very few admirers at that time, and I started corresponding with her in 1957; but I didn't meet her until 1964; and as a result I did almost nothing to help her during a long period of excruciating difficulty.

It was not, perhaps, her very worst time. That must have been the last three years of the forties, when she and her third husband, Max Hamer, were living at Beckenham in Kent, their money had run out, and Max, a retired naval officer, became so desperate that he stumbled into deep trouble which ended in a three-year prison sentence for trying to obtain money by fraudulent means. During that nightmare Jean, paralysed by depression, could do nothing but drink herself into a state so bad that she, too, was several times in court and once in jail. By the time we were in touch Max had served his sentence, they had crept away to a series of miserable lodgings in Cornwall, and Jean was no longer quite at rock-bottom; but she still had nine terribly difficult years ahead of her before re-emerging as a writer.

She had always been a very private person, but she was known in literary circles when her fourth novel, *Good Morning, Midnight*, came out in 1939. When the war began a lot of people 'disappeared' in that they were carried away from their natural habitat on joining the forces or taking up war-work. Jean followed her second husband out of London, so when he died, and she slithered with Max into their misfortunes, she was no longer in touch with former acquaintances and became 'lost'. Francis tried to find out what had happened to her and was told by one person that she had drowned herself in the Seine, by another that she had drunk herself to death. People expected that kind of fate for her.

It was the BBC which found her, when they were preparing to broadcast an adaptation of *Good Morning, Midnight* made and performed by the actress Selma vaz Dias. They advertised for information about 'the late Jean Rhys', and she answered. Learning of this, Francis wrote to her, and she replied, saying that she was working on a new book. Responding to Francis's and my enthusiasm, André Deutsch agreed that we should buy the option to see it – for £25.

When people exclaim at how mean this was I no longer blush simply because I have blushed so often. I tell myself that the pound bought much more in the fifties than it does now, which is true; that this was not, after all, an advance, only an advance on an advance, which is true; and that no one else in those days would have paid much more for an option, and that, too, is true. But it is inconceivable that anyone would have paid less – so mean it was. If we had known anything about Jean's circumstances I am sure that Francis and I would have fought for more, but it would be a long time before we gained any idea of them.

The trouble was, she kept up a gallant front. In the letters we exchanged between 1957, when she said that her book would be finished in 'six or nine months', and March 1966, when she announced that it *was* finished, she would refer to being held up by domestic disasters such as leaking pipes, or mice in the kitchen, and she would make the disasters sound funny. Not until I met her did I understand that for Jean such incidents were appalling: they knocked her right out because her inability to cope with life's practicalities went beyond anything I ever saw in anyone generally taken to be sane. Max's health had given out, but her loyalty to him extended beyond keeping silent about his prison sentence to disguising his subsequent helplessness. It was years before I learnt how dreadful her seventies had been as she alternated between the struggle to nurse him and bleak loneliness when he was in hospital. She ate too little, drank too much, was frightened, exhausted and ill – and paranoid into the bargain, seeing the village of Cheriton FitzPaine (to which they moved during these years) as a cruel place. So any little horror on top of all this would incapacitate her for weeks. And when it passed a certain point she would crack.

For example: she told me that neighbours were saying that she was a witch, and she told it lightly, so that I thought she was making a funny story out of some small incident. But Mr Woodward, the rector, was to say that indeed she had been so accused, and that anyone who thought such beliefs were extinct didn't know Devon. Jean, driven frantic, had run out into the road and attacked the woman who originated the charge with a pair of scissors, which led to her being bundled for a week or so into a mental hospital. 'And if you ask me,' said Mr Greenslade, one of her few friends in the village, as he drove me from Exeter in his taxi, 'it was the other one who ought to have been shut up, not poor Mrs Hamer.' And not a word of all that appeared in her letters.

Luckily she gradually became less inhibited with Francis – partly, no doubt, because he was a man, and partly because he wrote to her as a friend from his own home, not as her publisher from an office (he worked with us only part-time). To him she owed the fact that a publisher was waiting for her book, and in him (this was probably more important to her) she had found someone who understood and loved her writing, who was sympathetic, amusing, kind, anxious to help. He made her dig out stories and found magazines to publish them, and when at last she let him know that she was on the verge of collapse, he sent her £100 so that she could go to a hotel or into a nursing-home for a rest. Her letters to me during those years are those of a writer glad to have a sympathetic editor; her letters to Francis are those of someone luxuriating in the unexpected discovery of a friend. Had it not been for his support she would not have been able to finish the book through which, in spite of such heavy odds against it, she was slowly, slowly, slowly inching her way.

People are not, thank God, wholly explicable. Carole Angier's biography of Jean does as much as anything ever will to explain the connections between the life and the work, but how this hopelessly inept, seemingly incomplete woman could write with such clarity, power and grace remains a mystery. I have long since settled for this fact; but I think I have reached a better understanding of the bad-at-life side of Jean since coming to know Dominica*, the island in the eastern Caribbean where she was born.

I have been given an unusually close view of the island by a piece of great good fortune: becoming friends (through having been Jean's publisher) with a Dominican family which includes the man who knows more than anyone else about every aspect of it. In Lennox Honychurch one of the Caribbean's smallest islands has produced the region's best historian, and it is through mental spectacles borrowed from him that I suddenly saw how *foreign* Jean was when she came to England in 1906, at the age of sixteen.

The British, thinking 'West Indies', mostly envisage a mixture of Jamaica and Barbados with a touch of Mustique. My own image, which I considered well-founded because I had been there, was Trinidad & Tobago plus Jamaica. So Dominica surprised me.

In the first place, no one had seriously wanted to make a colony of it. Columbus hit on it in 1493, and once described it by scrunching up a sheet of paper and tossing it onto a table: an inadequate image, but one can see what he meant. It consists of thirty by sixteen miles of densely packed volcanic mountains separated by deep valleys into which waterfalls roar and down which little rivers, often turbulent, run. The whole of it is clad in exuberant forest and some of it is given to steaming and shuddering. The dramatic nature of its conformation, and the tropical richness of its forest (much of it rain forest) make it wonderfully beautiful, but it is hardly *useful-looking*.

Human beings have two ways of relating to such terrain. If, like

---

* Dominica has adopted the appellation 'The Commonwealth of Dominica'. The Dominican Republic, also in the Caribbean, is a different country, which shares an island with Haiti.

the Caribs, who were there when Columbus turned up, you are the kind of human who lives with nature rather than on or against it, you find it hospitable: you can't freeze in it, you can't starve in it, there is plenty of material for building shelters and a vast number of mighty trees out of which to make canoes; and if hostile humans invade they find it extremely difficult to move about in, while you can very easily hide, and then ambush them. (There are still more Caribs living in Dominica than anywhere else, and it enabled escaped slaves to put up a more impressive resistance to vengeful slave-owners than they could do on any other island.) But if you are the kind of human who likes to control nature, and hopes to make a profit from it, then you must either leave such an island alone, as the Spanish sensibly did, or else steel yourself to work very hard for sadly little return. Dominica's settlers have tried planting a variety of crops – coffee, cocoa, a very little sugar (not enough flat ground), lots of bananas and citrus fruit, vanilla, bay rum . . . all of them reasonably profitable for a time, then wiped out or greatly reduced by hurricanes, blights, or shifts in the market. In many parts of the Caribbean planters made fortunes; in Dominica with luck you got by, but rich you did not get.

It was the French who first, early in the eighteenth century, edged themselves in to start plantation life: the Dominicans of today, almost all of them of African descent, still speak the French-based patois introduced by the slaves of the French planters, and Catholicism remains the island's predominant religion. The English took the place over in 1763 as part of the peace settlement at the end of the Seven Years War between France and England, and were not excited by it. 'These islands', said a booklet for investors in 1764, 'are not the promised land, flowing with milk and honey . . . Of those who adventure, many fall untimely. Of those who survive, many fall before enjoyment ...'* Most plantation owners from then on were absentees who left managers in charge – men who had a bad reputation. A coffee planter in the eighteenth century wrote: 'When we look around and see the many drunken, ignorant, illiterate, dissolute, unprincipled Characters to whom the charge of property is confided ... it is no wonder that the Estate goes to ruin and destruction.' But the managers deserve some sympathy: it was a lonely life. The small and rustic estate houses were separated from each other not by great distances, but by impassable terrain.

To this day the abruptness with which mountains plunge into sea at each end of the island has defeated road-builders, so that no road runs right round it; and only since 1956 has it been possible to drive obliquely across it from the Caribbean to the Atlantic on a road forced by mountains to be much longer than the distance straight across. This trans-insular road, grandly named the Imperial Road, was officially 'opened' in about 1900, but in fact petered out halfway across, with only the first five or six miles surfaced. In Jean's day you either sailed round the island, or rode a very difficult track often interrupted by flood or landslip. Even the flat coast road linking Roseau and Portsmouth, the two main towns on the Caribbean side, was non-existent until 1972. Nowadays a few narrow metalled roads run up into the mountains from the coast, so that farmers can truck their produce down to be shipped; but when Jean went to visit her grandmother at Geneva, the family's estate, she rode nine miles of stony track.

Except for the one between Roseau and Portsmouth, Dominica's

---

* I owe both this and the next quotation to Lennox Honychurch's *The Dominica Story*.

narrow bumpy roads still inspire awe just by existing: so much forest to be cleared, so many ups and so many downs to be negotiated hairpin after hairpin after hairpin, so many tropical downpours to wash away what has just been achieved . . . and so little money and no earth-moving equipment! They are valiant little roads, and keeping them in repair is a heavy task.

So it is not surprising that few white people settled in Dominica. In Jean's girlhood an energetic Administrator tempted in a new generation of English planters, and briefly the white population soared . . . from forty-four in 1891 to three hundred and ninety-nine in 1911*. But the new planters soon gave up, and now it is under a dozen. Jean's parents lent her elder sister to rich relations to be brought up, and I can see why. White middle-class girls didn't work, they got married, and who was there in Dominica for a girl to marry? No one. In those days British neglect of the island had been so scandalous regarding schools that hardly any black Dominicans had any schooling at all. Racial prejudice would, anyway, have made a black husband for a white girl seem impossible, but there would also have been real incompatibility. White education was nothing to boast of, but even the least polished white daughter could read.

In a colonial society people only had to be white to feel themselves upper-class, in addition to which they hung on with determination to awareness of gentlemanly forebears if they had them, as the Lockharts (Jean's mother's family) did. So normal life to the child Jean was life at the top of the pile. Against which, the pile was no more than a molehill. Such a very small and isolated

---

* Figures from Peter Hulme's essay 'Islands and Roads', *The Jean Rhys Review*.

white society was less than provincial – less, even, than parochial, since there was considerably less enduring structure to it than to an average English village. It was threatened from below, which Jean sensed while still very young; but that pushed her in the direction of her family's attitudes, rather than away from them (not until she had worked her way through to the writer in herself – the seeing eye – would she, almost in spite of herself, reflect back an image of white Dominican society as it really was). As she approached the age of sixteen, when she would leave for England, her life was that of a tiny group of people whose experience was considerably narrower than they liked to think, combined with life in the head: dream life.

Part of the dream was of Dominica itself, because its combination of beauty and untameability exerts a strong pull on the imagination. Jean wrote*

> . . . It was alive, I was sure of it. Behind the bright colours
> the softness, the hills like clouds and the clouds like
> fantastic hills. There was something austere, sad, lost, all
> these things. I wanted to identify myself with it, lose myself
> in it. (But it turned its head away, indifferent, and that broke
> my heart.)
>   The earth was like a magnet which pulled me and
> sometimes I came near it, this identification or annihilation
> that I longed for. Once, regardless of the ants, I lay down
> and kissed the earth and thought, 'Mine, mine.' I wanted to
> defend it from strangers . . .

---

* In *Smile Please*, her last book. The writing is less taut and evocative than it used to be.

Outsiders, too, respond to it romantically. I know others beside myself who try to play down the intensity of their infatuation with it for fear of seeming absurd. I was charmed by Tobago, but it did not haunt my imagination as Dominica does. Perhaps it has to do with its volcanic nature. In addition to the Boiling Lake, steaming and gulping in its impressive crater, it has several lesser fumaroles, sulphur springs, earth tremors . . . vulcanologists say that at least four of its centres of volcanic activity might blow at any time. The inconceivable violence barely contained within our planet can't be forgotten on Dominica. It is a place so far from ordinary in the mind's eye that belonging to it, as Jean so passionately felt she did, must set one apart.

Her other dream was of England, bred partly from the way that colonial families of British origin idealized it, more from the books which were sent her by her grandmother on her father's side. From this material she created a promised land even more seductive than her beloved Dominica. Her father had an inkling of what would happen when she got there: he warned her that it would be 'very different', and told her to write directly to him if she was unhappy – 'But don't write at the first shock or I'll be disappointed in you.' But when they said goodbye, and he hugged her tightly enough to break the coral brooch she was wearing, she was unmoved by his emotion and felt very cheerful, 'for already I was on my way to England'. At which she arrived knowing so little about it that she might have been landing from Mars.

It was not just a matter of the obvious ignorances, such as not knowing what a train looked like (put into a little brown room at her first railway station she didn't realize what it was), or supposing that the hot water gushing from bathroom taps was inexhaustible (she was scolded for using it all up when she took her first bath, and how could she have known?). And of course she had never dreamt of endless streets of joined-together brick houses, all grey . . . All that was bad enough, but worse was having none of the instinctive sense of give and take that is gained from living in a complex society surrounded by plenty of people like oneself. The older women she had known had been given no more opportunity than she had to acquire this . . . She could hardly have known what it was that she lacked, but she did know how badly she was at a loss.

In England *everyone she met* knew things she didn't know – not just the things taught in schools, but baffling ordinary, everyday things. Many young women are nimble face-savers, able to learn ways out of difficult situations, but Jean was not. Already, for whatever reason, she was in some ways trammelled in childishness; already paranoia threatened. It did not occur to her to learn, all she could do was hate. She hated this country which was so far from resembling her dream, and even more fiercely its inhabitants, for despising (as she was sure they did) her ignorance and her home. This feeling persisted into her old age: I saw it flare up when a woman spoke of Castries, in St Lucia, as 'a shanty town'. Instantly Jean assumed that this sneering woman – these sneering English – would see Roseau in the same way, and Roseau was not a shanty town – it was *not* – they were not seeing it right. She sprang to defend it against strangers – hateful strangers. She had always hated them with their damned cold competence and common sense: never would she dream of trying to be like them. Probably she could not have been, anyway; but her abhorrence of what she saw as Englishness did make her *embrace* her own incompetence.

The book she was trying against such heavy odds to finish was

inspired by this hate. At first it was called 'The First Mrs Rochester'.
Charlotte Brontë's *Jane Eyre* had always filled her with indignation
on behalf of the mad West Indian wife shut up in the attic of
Thornfield Hall. She knew that Englishmen had sometimes married West Indian heiresses for their money, and suspected that
Brontë had based her story on local gossip about such a marriage;
and to Jean such gossip could only have been spiteful and unfair.
For years she had wanted to write a novel showing the wife's point
of view, and for almost as many years again that was what – with
long and painful interruptions – she had been doing.

We had not been corresponding for long before she admitted
that her worry about Part Two of *Wide Sargasso Sea* (as it had
become) was exhausting her. In this Part Mr Rochester turns up
and marries Antoinette (disliking the name Bertha, which Brontë
gave the wife, Jean chooses to call her heroine by her second name).
Their relationship has to be established and the reason why this
marriage of convenience goes so terribly wrong has to be explained.
For Antoinette's childhood and schooling, Jean said in letters, she
could draw on her own, and 'the end was also possible because I *am*
in England and can all too easily imagine being mad'. But for the
wedding and what followed she had nothing to go on, and she
went through agonies of uncertainty: 'Not one real fact. Not one.
No dialogue. Nothing.'

She sent an early version of Parts One and Two to Francis, who
showed them to me, and in that version Part Two was indeed thin:
the marriage became a disaster almost immediately, before it had
been given time to exist. About this I wrote to her – nervously,
because Part One was so marvellous that the book I was meddling
with could obviously become a work of genius. I was relieved when
she accepted what I had said; but not until much later, when I read

one of her letters to Francis*, did I see that my suggestion had been of real use.

She told him of certain 'clues' that had led her forward. The first was obeah, and how it must have played its ambiguous part in the story. 'The second clue was when Miss Athill suggested a few weeks' happiness for the unfortunate couple – before he gets disturbing letters.' Starting to follow this suggestion, she saw at once that 'He must have fallen for her, and violently too', and at once the marriage came alive and was launched on its complex and agonizing course.

That was to remain my only editorial intervention, strictly speaking, in Jean Rhys's work: on points of detail she was such a perfectionist that she never needed 'tidying up'.

Jean and I met for the first time in November 1964, when, after the support she had received from Francis, and also from another Deutsch editor, Esther Whitby, who had volunteered to spend a weekend at Cheriton FitzPaine to help her sort out and arrange what she had written, she felt able to bring the finished book to London. Or rather, the almost finished book: there were still a few lines which she would have to dictate to the typist to whom we had given the material brought back by Esther. We would meet, Jean and I, for a celebratory lunch the day after she arrived . . . Instead, I was called to her hotel by an agitated manageress, who reported that she had suffered a heart attack during the night. So there was no triumph over a bottle of champagne. I had to pack her into an ambulance and take her to hospital. This, followed by three or four weeks of hospital visiting, with all the usual intimacies of

* In *Jean Rhys: Letters 1931–1966*, edited by Francis Wyndham and Diana Melly, André Deutsch, 1984.

nightdress washing, toothpaste buying and so on, plunged us into the deep end of friendship – though I soon learnt that it would be a mistake to suppose that meant trust. Jean never entirely trusted anybody. But she was never thereafter to show me an unfriendly face.

At the end of her first day in hospital she presented me with what might have become a painful moral problem: she asked me for a solemn promise that the book would never be published in its unfinished state – without, that is, the few lines she had been intending to dictate. Naturally I gave it. And then I went home to think 'What if she dies?'. It seemed quite likely that she would. The book was publishable as it stood – perhaps a footnote or two would be necessary at the places where the lines were to go, but that was all. If she died would I be able to – would it even be right to – keep my promise? Now I know there would have been no question about it: of course we would have published. But at the time, in all the disturbance and anxiety caused by her illness, my sense of the terrifyingly treacherous world in which Jean's paranoia could trap her (I'd picked that up at once) was so strong that I felt any promise given her *must* be real.

A possible solution occurred to me. Esther had described how Jean kept her manuscript in shopping-bags under her bed, a hugger-mugger of loose sheets and little notebooks which Jean had said only she herself could make sense of. I knew that her brother, Colonel Rees-Williams, was coming up from Budleigh Salterton to visit her in hospital. Why not ask him to collect every bag of writing he could find in her cottage and bring it to me, without telling her (she was too ill to deal with it herself)? I would then go through it, returning everything meticulously to the order in which I found it, hoping to find clues to what she intended to insert; so that, if the worst happened, I could follow, at least approximately, her intentions.

Colonel Rees-Williams did his part, but in vain. Jean had been right: she *was* the only person who could make sense of the amazing muddle seething in those bags. So I gave up, her brother put the bags back exactly where he found them, and Jean never knew what we had done.

It took her nearly two years to regain enough strength to look at the book again, and to add the scraps of material she felt to be necessary. She could do it, she said, because of a new pill prescribed, I think, by a new doctor – though it may have been her old doctor trying something new. Perhaps he was the most important contributor to the conclusion of that novel, so I am sorry I cannot name him.

It was on March 9th 1966 that she wrote to tell me that the book was finished – and that Max was dead.

My dear Diana

Thank you for your letter [knowing that Max was dying I had just written her a letter of affection and anxiety]. I don't know what else to say. Max died unconscious, and this morning very early we went to Exeter crematorium.

A sunny day, a *cold* sun, and a lot of flowers but it made no sense to me.

I feel that I've been walking a tight rope for a long time and have finally fallen off. I can't believe that I am so alone and there is no Max.

I've dreamt several times that I was going to have a baby – then I woke with relief.

Finally I dreamt that I was looking at the baby in a cradle – such a puny weak thing.

So the book must be finished, and that must be what I
think about it really. I don't dream about it any more.
Love from Jean

It's so *cold*.

I asked if I could come to Cheriton to collect the book, which
seemed to please her; that first visit was when Mr Greenslade, sent
by Jean to pick me up at Exeter, told me about her attack on her
disagreeable neighbour.

She had booked me a room at the Ring of Bells, the village pub,
because although she had a tiny extra room it would be another
two years before it was inhabitable. Her letters always bewailed the
weather, and sure enough, when I walked the length of the village
to Landboat Bungalows, where she lived in number 6, it was rain-
ing and windy; and the village, too, behaved as she always said it
did. On a walk of about half a mile I saw not a single person, the
houses all stood with their backsides to the road, and the two dogs
I met – mongrels of a sheepdog type – peered at me with hostile
yellow eyes through their sodden shagginess and sidled away as
though they expected me to stone them. Later I would see Cheriton
looking quite normal (though the houses turning their backs to the
road on that stretch of it remained odd); but that day I thought
'What a depressing place – she hasn't been exaggerating at all'.

I had always thought of a bungalow as a detached dwelling sitting
on its own little plot, but Jean's was the last in a joined-together row
of one-storey shacks, crouching grey, makeshift and neglected behind
a hedge which almost hid them. They looked as though corrugated
iron, asbestos and tarred felt were their main ingredients, and if I had
been told that I must live in one of them I would have been appalled.

Jean could not afford to heat, and so didn't use, the only decent room which, like her bedroom, looked out over what would have been the garden had it been cultivated, towards some fields. On the road side there was a strip of rough grass shaded by the hedge, and the door opened into a narrow unlit passage, bathroom on the left, kitchen – into which I was immediately steered – on the right. It was about ten feet by ten, and it was just as well that it was no bigger; the only heating, apart from the two-burner gas cooker, was an electric heater of the kind which has little bars in front of a concave metal reflector, which scorches the shins of the person just in front while failing to warm the space as a whole. The small table at which Jean worked and ate, two upright chairs, a cupboard for food and another for utensils were all the furniture, and this was the room in which Jean spent all day, every day.

I doubt whether she could have survived another year in Landboat Bungalows if she had not managed to finish *Wide Sargasso Sea*.

Its publication, followed by the reissue of all her earlier work except for two or three stories which she didn't consider good enough to keep, brought her money: not a great deal of it, but enough to keep her warm and comfortable for the rest of her life. It also brought her fame, to which she was almost completely indifferent but which must have been better than being forgotten, and friends. Among the friends was Sonia Orwell, who made more difference to her life than anyone else.

Sonia struck me as tiresome. She often drank too much, was easily bored, which made her tetchy and sometimes rude, and was an intellectual snob without having, as far as I could see, a good enough mind to justify it. But although I suspect it was Jean's sudden fame, rather than her writing in itself, which made Sonia take her up, once she had been moved to do so she was amazingly generous about it.

She financed long winter holidays in London for Jean every year from the publication of *Wide Sargasso Sea* in 1966 to the end of her life, and she gave her many expensive presents. When I remarked on the amount she was spending she told me that she had always felt embarrassed at having inherited George Orwell's literary income, and had decided that she must use it to help writers who were hard up. This she said shyly and apologetically, to stop me thinking she was more generous than she was, not to take credit for it. And more impressive than the money she spent was the sensitivity she showed in her determination to give Jean a good time. She didn't just pay hotel bills: she did all the tipping in advance, she explained to the management the special kinds of attention this old lady would need, she booked hairdressers and manicurists, she bought pretty dressing-gowns, she saw to it that the fridge was full of white wine and of milk for Jean's nightcap, she supplied books, she organized visitors . . . From time to time she even did the thing she most hated (as I did too): took Jean shopping for clothes. This was so exhausting and so boring that eventually we both went on strike – and it was Sonia who then saw to it that younger and stronger spirits took our place. It was also she who was the most active member of what we called 'the Jean Committee' – the meetings at which she, Francis and I discussed 'Jean problems', such as getting her finances in order, or trying to find her somewhere to live nearer London, and less mingy, than Landboat Bungalows. (In this we did not succeed: whenever we came up with a real possibility Jean would jib: 'Better the devil I know', she would say.)

*

My gratitude for all this was profound, because quite early on I had been faced with a daunting prospect.

Jean loved her daughter, Maryvonne Moerman. She longed for her visits, grieved when she left, talked about her often with pride and admiration. During her bad times she had never burdened Maryvonne with worrying facts, and when she had money she constantly pondered ways of leaving her as much of it as possible. Several times she asked me to find answers to questions about the inheritance of money from England by someone living in Holland, as the Moermans did after returning from some years in Indonesia; and she often spoke about writing an account for Maryvonne of how the past had really been. If she could get it right, she said, then Maryvonne would at last understand.

What was it that she so urgently wanted her daughter to understand – and, by unmistakable implication, to forgive?

How much of Maryvonne's infancy was spent with her mother I do not know exactly, but I think it was almost none. Certainly she was for a time in 'a very good home run by nuns', and other nurseries were also involved. Fairly soon after her birth Jean got a job ghost-writing an autobiography in the south of France, one of its attractions being that if it worked she would be able to have her baby with her – but it didn't work. And when Maryvonne was about four years old Jean went away to England, leaving her to be raised in Holland by her father. Maryvonne adored her father, and arrangements were made later for her to spend school holidays in England with Jean, which she remembers as enjoyable: but it is hard for any small child not to feel, if her mother vanishes, that she has been abandoned.

This Jean could never undo, whatever she wrote, because the person she wanted forgiveness from was the abandoned child.

Maryvonne the grown-up woman understood very well that she
must accept her mother's nature – her absolute inability to behave
like a capable adult in the face of practical difficulties – and she was
generous enough to forgive it; but nothing could change what
Maryvonne the child had experienced. This cruel fact brought Jean
to a halt each time she approached it, and did more than the weakness of old age to explain why *Smile Please*, the autobiography she
attempted in her late eighties, ended where it did. And no doubt it
was this haunt between them that caused Maryvonne's longed-for
visits always to end in some kind of pain and bitterness.

So after one of her visits to Cheriton, Maryvonne came to
London and asked me to lunch with her. Jean had been talking of
moving to Holland, and Maryvonne had decided that she must
quickly establish that this was impossible. She told me that she
would keep in touch with her mother and visit her from time to
time, and that I could count on her to come over in an emergency,
but that she could not have her with or near her all the time. I
would have to take on the responsibility of looking after Jean,
because she simply couldn't do it. 'It would wreck my marriage,' she
said.

I cannot deny that my heart sank, all the more so because I
could see exactly what Maryvonne meant. I knew less about Jean
then than I do now, but I knew enough to see that she could not be
lived with; certainly not by a daughter she had dumped at the age
of about four. All editors have, to some extent, to play the role of
Nanny, and I saw that in this case it was about to expand – in
terms of size, not of glamour – into a star part. And so it would
most onerously have done if it had not been for Sonia's invaluable
help, and that of Francis. But he was soon to have his mother's old
age to deal with, so he had gradually to withdraw from practical

involvement, whereas it was many years before a combination of financial trouble and ill-health caused Sonia to flag.

It was thanks to her that I got a glimpse of how enchanting Jean must have been as a young woman (when happy). Sonia had taken her out to lunch and they had drunk enough champagne to make them both giggly – 'tipsy' would be the word rather than 'drunk'. When Jean got drunk (which I was not to witness until the last two years of her life) it was usually a disastrous release of resentment and rage; but this time her tipsiness hit the level which is exactly right. Everything became comic: she remembered – and sang – delightful songs; she told jokes; she liked everyone. She might have been enclosed in a pink bubble of Paris-when-she-was-happy-there, and it lasted until I had filled her hot water bottle and steered her into bed (I was taking the late afternoon and evening shift, as I usually did). Jean and I often spent enjoyable times together, but only with Sonia did she taste that sort of fun. Sonia, who knew Paris intimately, brought a whiff of Jean's favourite city with her, and she drank too much; whereas I was so undeniably English, and liked to stay sober. With me Jean couldn't quite let herself go.

That occasion was at the Portobello Hotel: the Portobello winter was the best of the treats provided by Sonia. The hotel was small, elegant in an informal way, and favoured by French theatre people. At that time it was being managed by a young woman recently celebrated in a Sunday newspaper as one of 'the new Fat' – a despiser of dieting who liked to wear flamboyant clothes and enjoy her own amplitude. She had, Sonia told me, made a special price for Jean because she loved her books (unfortunately she was no longer in charge when the next winter came round, perhaps because of her amiable tendency to make such gestures). The first time I visited

Jean there I was greeted at the reception desk by a faun-like being in a pink T-shirt trimmed with swansdown which had little zipped slits over each breast, both of them unzipped so that his nipples peeped out. This seemed such a far cry from Cheriton FitzPaine that I wondered whether Jean, much as she longed for a change, would find it upsetting; but she loved it, was fussed over charmingly by both the manageress and the saucy faun, and would have been happy to spend the rest of her days at the Portobello. I think it was during that holiday that she played with the idea of dyeing her hair red. I protested, because bright hair-dyes make one's skin look old, and she said: 'But it's not other people I want to fool – only myself.'

Where Jean was *not* happy was in a hotel which Sonia fell back on later, when she was beginning to feel the financial pinch which, together with illness, made her last years miserable. It was one of those comfortable but drab places near the Cromwell Road which are chosen as permanent homes by elderly widows, and Jean made her loathing of it brutally clear. Generosity inspired in her no more sense of obligation than it would have done in a six-year-old, and even after Sonia had moved her (as she quickly did) into a vastly chic and expensive establishment, she remained slightly sulky. It was to Sonia, not to her, that the manager of the rejected hotel had said that they were accustomed to – indeed, specialized in – elderly people, but Jean had picked it up the moment she crossed the threshold, and was not going to forgive the making of such a choice for her. Later still, when Sonia left London for a cheaper life in Paris, I and others often explained to Jean how her circumstances had changed. Jean would acknowledge her friend's misfortunes with a ritual 'Poor Sonia', but her voice would be indifferent and there would be a distant look in her eyes. For her, inevitably, a friend who had gone away was a friend who was rejecting her.

Jean's comparative sedateness with me made it a shock when I received a letter from a man who had been her neighbour in Beckenham, and who resented the acclaim she was getting for *Wide Sargasso Sea*. He wrote an unsparing, and horridly convincing, description of the aggressive drunken behaviour which had led to her arrests, and he also took it on himself to tell me about Max's disaster, which Jean had never mentioned. I was able, therefore, to explain Jean's lapses as a breakdown under strain. Only in her last few years did I begin to understand that ugly drunkenness had been her downfall, on and off, for most of her adult life. Before that, my personal experience of her had revealed her incompetence, her paranoia, her need for help and reassurance, and the superficial nature of her gratitude ('I've got hold of some money' was how she told Maryvonne of Francis's gift, and glimpses of that attitude were not infrequent through the chinks in her politeness). But I also knew that she was very often charming, had an old-fashioned sense of decorum and good taste (she hated unkind gossip), and that however tiresome her muddles could be, I enjoyed being her nanny more often than I found it wearisome.

It did not really matter that the Jean Committee failed to find her a new house. Her bungalow was made so much more comfortable and pleasant by the hard work and ingenuity of two of her new friends, Jo Batterham and Gini Stevens, that – given more visitors, and the daily help which Sonia and I were at last able to find for her – she was probably as well off there as anywhere. Gini even took over the role of amanuensis for a while (Jean couldn't type and was frightened of tape-recorders, so she always had to have that kind of help). Like so many of Jean's relationships, this one ended in tears; but not before it had enabled her to put together the collection of stories, *Sleep it Off, Lady*, which would have been impossible without it.

Meanwhile Jean's finances were, by a miracle, kept in order by an accountant recommended by Sonia on the grounds that he liked good writing and drank a lot.

A good example of a Jean muddle was the case of Selma vaz Dias, the actress who had adapted *Good Morning, Midnight* for the radio, and who saw herself, not without reason, as Jean's true 'rediscoverer'. The trouble with Selma was not that she made that claim, but that she thought herself entitled by it to become a bandit.

Although middle-aged and rather stout, she was a striking woman with bold dark eyes who wore clothes to suggest a dash of the Spanish gypsy, and was an ebullient talker. Jean had been delighted and grateful on learning of her plans for *Good Morning, Midnight*, had enjoyed her company when they met, and loved her infrequent letters. Knowing they had planned to meet when Jean brought the manuscript of *Wide Sargasso Sea* to London, I telephoned Selma to report that she had been taken to hospital . . . and began almost at once to doubt the worth of her friendship. First, a surprising amount of prodding was necessary to make her visit Jean; then the visit turned out to be extremely short and to consist mostly of Selma complaining of its inconvenience to herself; and lastly, when I was giving her a lift home after it, she said almost nothing about Jean except: 'You know, of course, that she used to work as a prostitute?'

Worse was to emerge. After the publication of *Wide Sargasso Sea* Jean confessed to worry about something which Selma had made her sign. It then came out that in 1963, on a visit to Cheriton, Selma had produced 'a bit of paper' which Jean understood to concern the broadcast rights of *Good Morning, Midnight*, *Voyage in the Dark* and *Wide Sargasso Sea*, but which was in fact an agreement to give Selma fifty per cent of the proceeds from any film, stage, television or radio adaptation of any of Jean's books, anywhere in the world, for so long as the books were in copyright, and granting Selma sole artistic control of any such adaptation. Jean was to say repeatedly that she thought being made to sign it was a joke – 'I was a bit drunk, you see . . . well, a bit, very.' However, two years later, when Selma got an agent to recast this same agreement in more formal terms, and he wrote to ask Jean whether she really did want to sign it again, she apparently felt that she must, and did so. (The agent had never met her, so I suppose was unaware of her near-idiocy in practical matters; otherwise he would, I hope, have taken a stronger line.)

At first I was not too worried, because I was unable to believe that anything so outrageous could stand. Selma herself, I thought, could surely be made to see as much: a foolish thought, that one turned out to be. Then André Deutsch and I talked to her husband who, though obviously deeply embarrassed, insisted there was nothing he could do. So – 'Write a full account of the whole thing,' said André to me, 'and I'll send it to Arnold.'

'Arnold' was Arnold Goodman, not yet a lord but already the most famous lawyer in the United Kingdom and André's guru. Hope revived: *of course* Arnold would save the day. But all he could say was that this was a contract, and if someone was daft enough to sign a contract without understanding it, whether drunk or sober, too bad for them. My inability to expect anything good from lawyers was born out of that day's impotent rage.

I have forgotten how I knew that the theatrical agent Margaret
Ramsay had once been Selma's agent and friend, but I did know it,
and inspiration hit me. 'If anyone can deal with this it will be that
little war-horse.' Peggy always talked without drawing breath, so
when she heard me name one of my authors it was a minute or two
before I could stem the torrent of her refusal even to think about
taking on another writer, and explain our problem. Once she had
taken it in: 'GOOD GOD! That's perfectly appalling! Selma can't be
allowed to get away with that. LEAVE HER TO ME!' Oh, the
gratitude.

Even Peggy couldn't make Selma cancel the contract, but she did
get her to reduce her fifty per cent to thirty-three and a third; and –
far more important – she did make her cancel the clause giving her
artistic control by somehow drilling into her mulish head that such
a clause would forever prevent the sale of any such rights to anyone.

From then on Peggy Ramsay handled all Jean's film, stage, television and radio rights; and a few years later we steered her other
literary affairs into the hands of the agent Anthony Sheil – a belated
and profound relief. Because until then almost anyone Jean met
could, and only too often did, become her agent, with results
which – though never so dire as the Selma affair – were often maddeningly confusing and counter-productive.

Although I never had to do any work on a text by Jean, I did once
intervene by discouraging the inclusion of one of her stories in the
collection *Sleep it Off, Lady*. Francis, too, advised her to leave it
out; I can't now remember which of us was the first to raise the
matter. In a catalogue of her private papers, appended to the type-
script of the story 'The Imperial Road', there is this note: 'Miss
Rhys has stated that her publishers declined to include this story in

Sleep it off, Lady, considering it to be too anti-Negro in tone.' True, but over-simplified.

Jean shared many of the attitudes of other white Dominicans born towards the end of the nineteenth century. It is true that she often spoke of how, as a child, she longed to be black, because black people's lives were so much less cramped by boring inhibitions than those of the whites; but this was a romantic rebellion within the existing framework, not a rejection of the framework. When I knew her she talked – sometimes unselfconsciously, sometimes with a touch of defiance – like any other old member of the Caribbean plantocracy, describing black people she liked as 'loyal'; saying what a mess 'they' had made of things once 'we' were no longer there (that was the burden of 'The Imperial Road') and so on. Typical white liberal of the sixties that I was, I disliked hearing her talk like that, but it seemed natural: and it never failed to make me marvel that in *Wide Sargasso Sea* she had, by adhering to her creed as a writer, transcended her own attitude.

Her creed – so simple to state, so difficult to follow – was that she must tell the truth: must get things down *as they really were*. Carole Angier, in her biography, has demonstrated how this fierce endeavour enabled her to write her way through to understanding her own damaged nature; and it also enabled her, in her last novel, to show Dominica's racial pain as it really was. But it didn't work in 'The Imperial Road'.

Oddly enough neither Francis nor I was then aware of how far it was from working. We were simply uneasy at the story's tone, without realizing that it was the consequence of a major (though explicable) misunderstanding on Jean's part. In the story the Jean-figure sets out to cross Dominica on the Imperial Road – the trans-insular road built in her childhood. Revisiting the island many years later she wants to follow the road. To her incredulous dismay she finds that 'they' have let it be swallowed up by the forest: it is no longer there.

Jean herself had been present, as a child, at the opening of the Imperial Road, and had not unnaturally supposed that if a trans-insular road is declared open, it must have been built. No one had explained to her that it had in fact been built only to a point half-way across, where the Administrator's estate happened to be, and that even that stretch of it was metalled for only five miles. What she thought, thirty years later, to have vanished as a result of 'their' neglect, had never in fact been built by 'us'. So the story was even more 'wrong' than it smelled to Francis and me; and once I had learnt the historical facts I became even gladder that she did not dig in her heels and insist on including it (which, of course, she could have done if she had really wanted to).

The contrast with *Wide Sargasso Sea* is striking. In that novel the story is told from the point of view of someone whose life was wrecked by the emancipation of the slaves, and who is puzzled and angry, as well as grieved, by the hostility which blacks are now free to show against whites. But because the observation is so precise, and the black and mixed-blood people are allowed their own voices when they speak, the reader understands why Coulibri is burnt down; why Daniel Cosway has become the very disagreeable person he is; why the child Tia turns against Antoinette – indeed, has never really been able to be her friend, which is a fact equally cruel to both of them. Antoinette's world has been poisoned, not by these people's malice, but by their having been owned, until very recently, by her family as though they were cattle. Nowhere does Jean say this, but she shows it: Jean writing at her best knew more than the

Jean one met in everyday life. I did not want her to publish 'The Imperial Road' because I did not want anyone to despise as racist a writer who could, when it mattered, defeat her own limitations with such authority.

By the time Jean started work on her last book, the autobiographical *Smile Please*, she was too old to do without help; but it was not I who gave it (apart from reading and making encouraging noises as it progressed) . . . She had always had to find someone to type her books for her, and continued to think of the person helping her as doing no more than that. But the novelist David Plante, who had offered to be her amanuensis for this book, did a good deal more to coax material out of her, and organize it, than she acknowledged. There was an anxious time when she panicked at what he was doing, telling me that he was taking the book over and trying to make it his own; but he had only been using scissors and paste on a few pages, to get the material into its proper sequence. Once she had been persuaded to read it and see her own words still saying what she wanted them to say, she relaxed. More or less. That was a difficult time: her last winter in London, when she proved to be beyond coping with a hotel, and Diana Melly, with incomparable generosity, took her into her house (indeed, gave up her own bedroom to her) for three months. After a few weeks of great pleasure, Jean began to slide into a sort of senile delinquency, and to drink too much: one of David's problems was steering his way between the disintegration which soon followed if he joined her in a drink, and the mutinous rage if he refused to. I remember huddling round the kitchen table with him and Diana, all of us agreeing that it was just a matter of one of us going upstairs and *taking the drinks tray out of her room* . . . a discussion which ended in Diana saying: 'Oh God – we're none of us any more use than a wet Kleenex.' But the book did get done, all the same: it was not what she wanted it to be, but it had a good deal more value than she feared.

In fact *Smile Please* is an extraordinary example of Jean's ability to condense: everything about her that matters is in it, though sometimes touched in so lightly that it can escape the notice of a reader who is less than fully attentive. It was as though something in her quite separate from her conscious mind was still in control, still making choices and decisions; and I have always thought that, about a year earlier, I was granted a glimpse of that something at work.

The proofs of *Sleep it Off, Lady* came in from the printer while Jean was in London, and she told me she was worried about checking them because she feared she was no longer capable of the necessary concentration. So I suggested that I should read them aloud to her, going very slowly, and doing no more than twenty minutes at a time. As soon as we began she became a different person, her face stern, her eyes hooded, her concentration intense. When I was halfway down the first galley-proof she said: 'Wait – go back to the beginning – it must be about three lines down – where it says "and then". Put a full stop instead of the "and", and start a new sentence.' She was carrying the whole thing in her mind's eye.

This tiny incident seemed to me to give a clear glimpse of the central mystery of Jean Rhys: the existence within a person so incompetent and so given to muddle and disaster – even to destruction – of an artist as strong as steel.

It was that incident which made me write the following lines, which I think of as 'Notes for a biography which will never be written'.

<u>THE MOTHER</u> A woman wearing corsets under a dark
serge riding habit, cantering over sand under palm trees, up
a track through the forest of leaves like hands, saws, the ears
of elephants.

She banished mangoes from the breakfast table and gave
her children porridge, lumpy because it was cooked by
long-fingered brown hands more adept at preparing
calaloo. She made the children wear woollen underwear the
colour of porridge.

'What will become of you?' she said.

For all her care they were in danger of not seeming English.
Her grandfather had built his house in the forest and taken
a beautiful wife whose hair was straight and fell to her waist.
But it, and her eyes, were very black.

Only one child was pink and white, with blue eyes, the
proof. Why was she the one so difficult to love?

That child never asked and never told. She listened hungrily
to the laughter in the kitchen, was locked in sulky silence
when the Administrator's wife came to tea, and let the eyes
of old men dwell on her.

'What will become of you?' Addressed to this one the
question was more urgent, even angry; and after a while was
not asked because what was the good? Who is not annoyed
and fatigued by perversity?

But the child obeyed her mother. Bidden to dream of England, she dreamt. 'When I get there,' she dreamt, 'it will be like the poems, not like she says.' When she got there she found dark serge, porridge and porridge-coloured underwear. 'My poor mother,' she said later. She had decided long ago never to forgive a country's whole population, so she could afford to say no more than that about one woman.

THE FATHER A man in a panama hat and a white linen suit, leaving the house to make people better. 'Is the doctor in?' The voices were sometimes frightened and only he could help. He was often out, often had to be spared trouble when he was in, so it was a long time before he came into the room and found the child crying over her plate of lumpy porridge. 'In this climate!' he said. And after that her breakfast was an egg beaten up in milk, flavoured with sugar and nutmeg.

He liked her to mix his evening drink, and as she carefully measured out the rum and lime juice, and grated a little nutmeg over the glass, she knew she was a pretty sight in her white frock which hid the woollen vest.

It was his mother who sent the child books for Christmas and all the grown-up books in the glass-fronted case were his, except *The Sorrows of Satan* which was her mother's. And when he was a boy he ran away to sea because people were unkind and he couldn't bear it.

When he died there was no more money and no more love, and no one, she saw after that, could be relied on. But: 'I have always been grateful to my father,' she said later, 'because he showed me that if you can't bear something it's all right to run away.'

<u>THEIR DAUGHTER</u> She didn't want to hurt the man, but she went with him. Her new dream was Paris and he could take her there. He came at a time when her bad luck was so bad that she deserved a little good luck for a change. She thought: 'Poor man, I am sorry about this, but I would have been done for if he had not turned up to make life less difficult.'

She didn't want the child to die, but when it went a strange colour and wouldn't eat she thought: 'This baby, poor thing, has gone a strange colour and won't eat and I don't know what to do. I'm no good at this.' So she took it to a hospital and left it there. When they wrote to tell her it had died she saw that life was as cruel as she had always believed. But it did become less difficult.

She wanted to keep the other child, but where could she have put her? How could she have fed her? She thought: 'Perhaps one day my luck will change and I will get her back.' Her luck did change, and after that she saw the child from time to time; but the child loved her father better than she loved her. That was unfair. But it did make life less difficult.

Cruelty had never surprised her because she had always heard it sniffing under the door; and the exhausting difficulty was her own fault. She knew that others who wanted blue skies, pretty dresses, kind men, went out to find what they wanted, but she was no good at that, she never had been. So all she could do was wait for her luck to change. And dream. 'If you dream hard enough, sometimes it comes true.' She could dream very hard, and when it failed to work she dreamt harder. But never hard enough to dream away one thing: her gift. She ran away, she dodged, she lay low, but her gift was always there. Over and over again it forced her to stand, to listen to the rattling door and put what she heard into words which were as nearly precisely true as she could make them. She said about her gift: 'I hate it, for making me good at this one thing which is so difficult.'

Perhaps she thought that true. She could not see herself when she was working. Out of her eyes, then, looked a whole and fearless being, without self-pity, knowing exactly what she wanted to do, and how to do it.

ALFRED CHESTER

IT IS POSSIBLE that I am the only person in the United Kingdom who remembers Alfred Chester and his books: what he wrote was too strange to attract a large readership, and we did not overcome this problem. But he remains the most remarkable person I met through publishing and I, and his friends in the United States who, since his death in 1971, have been finding new readers for him, continue to think and talk about knowing him as one of our most important experiences.

He was twenty-six when I first met him in 1956, the year we published his novel *Jamie Is My Heart's Desire* and his stories *Here Be Dragons*. First impressions? The very first was probably of ugliness – he wore a wig, his brows and eyelids were hairless, his eyes were pale, he was dumpy – but immediately after that came his openness and funniness. It didn't take me long to become fond of Alfred's appearance.

He also inspired awe, partly because of his prose and partly because of his personality. Alfred wore a wig, but never a mask:

there he sat, being Alfred, and there was nothing anyone could do about it. He was as compactly himself as a piece of quartz.

He had come to London from Paris, where he had been kicking up his heels in green meadows of freedom from his conventional, even philistine, Jewish family in Brooklyn. Already brilliant young New Yorkers such as Susan Sontag and Cynthia Ozick, who had known him when they were students together, were eyeing him nervously as one who might be going to outshine them, but he had needed to get away. And now he was in a stage of first-novel euphoria, ready to enjoy whatever and whoever happened. Meeting him, whether alone or at parties, reminded me of the excitement and alarm felt by Tolstoy's Natasha Rostov on meeting her seducer and knowing at once that between her and this man there were none of the usual barriers. Something like that shock of sexual accessibility can exist on the level of friendship: an instant recognition that with this person nothing need be hidden. I felt this with Alfred (though there was a small dark pit of secrecy in the middle of the openness: I would never have spoken to him about his wig).

On his second visit he was with his lover, a very handsome young pianist called Arthur. When I went to supper with them in the cave-like flat which they had rented or borrowed, Arthur spent much time gazing yearningly at a portrait of Liszt, and I wondered whether Alfred was husband or wife in this ménage (heterosexuals are always trying to type-cast homosexuals). I decided eventually that, on that evening, anyway, what he mostly was was Mother.

That was the first time he talked to me about identity, explaining how painful it was not to have one: to lack a basic 'I' and to exist only as a sequence of behaviours. Did I have a basic and continuous sense of identity, he asked, and I was tempted not to say 'Yes' because such a commonplace lack of anxiety seemed uninteresting compared with the condition he was claiming. I think I put the temptation aside because I didn't take him seriously. How could quartz-like Alfred feel, even for a second, that he had no basic identity?

Nevertheless I remember that long-ago talk very clearly. Perhaps I am being wise after the event, but it seems to me there was a slight judder of uneasiness under the surface which fixed it in my head.

Through '56 and '57 we exchanged letters, and one of his contained a passage which now seems obviously deranged.

I was running away from the police, through Luxembourg which is incredibly beautiful (a valley in the midst of a city), then to Brussels and back to Paris in thirty-six hours without sleep only to find that no one was chasing me after all. Unless they are being incredibly clever. You see, I'll be able to do things like that when I finish my book.

That sounds like paranoia. And how does the last sentence connect with the first two? But I was not much disturbed by this letter at the time. The rest of it was cheerful and normal, and the sobriety of my own life compared with Alfred's must have made me assume that his might well include mystifying events.

A letter of mine dated July 1959 reminds me that one of his London visits ended when he disappeared without a word.

. . . at one time, a long time ago, there was an extraordinary panic in London. John Davenport kept calling me and

Elizabeth Montagu kept calling me and I kept calling J.D. and E.M. and they kept calling each other and at one point an excursion was organised to Archway to confirm that you really had vanished and were not lying there sick unto death, or dead, or were not under arrest. After a while we said to each other 'Look, if any of those things had happened we'd have heard *somehow*. Wherever he is he must be all right.' So we gave up.

It was about a year after this disappearance that a visiting New Yorker let fall that Alfred was back in New York, and gave me the address to which I sent the above, whereupon Alfred replied that yes indeed, he'd become fed up with Greece and was now installed in a Greenwich Village apartment 'with a *roof garden*!'. And that was where I next saw him when I was on a business visit to New York: in almost unfurnished rooms above the theatre in Sullivan Street, where I found our friendship in good health.

Alfred had to lead the way up the stairs because he was feuding with the landlord who had taken to leaving brooms and buckets in the darkness, to trip him and send him crashing through the frail and wobbly banisters. As we climbed he described the feud with great relish. It was still daylight, so he took me right to the top to show me the roof garden – the heat-softened asphalt of the roof's surface, thickly studded with dog turds. Dutifully I leant over the parapet to admire the view and the freshness of the breeze, but I was shocked. Dogs are quasi-sacred in my family, and I had been raised in the understanding that they don't ask to belong to people, so – given that we have taken them over for our own pleasure – it is our duty not only to love them but to recognize their nature and treat them accordingly. Never have I denied a dog exercise and the chance to shit in decent comfort away from its lair – adult dogs, except for half-witted ones, dislike fouling their own quarters. I saw soon enough that Alfred's beloved Columbine and Skoura, whom he had rescued in Greece, were a barbaric pair, perfectly happy to shit on the roof – and indeed on the floors, and the mattresses which lay on the floors to serve as beds. They had never been house-trained, and Skoura, anyway, *was* half-witted. But still I was disconcerted that Alfred was prepared to inflict such a life on his dogs.

It was dark by the time we sat down by candlelight (the electricity may have been cut off) to eat mushrooms in sour cream and some excellent steak, and the dim light concentrated on the carefully arranged table disguised the room's bareness and dirt. Halfway through the meal we heard someone coming up the stairs. Alfred hushed me and blew out the candles. A knock, a shuffling, breathing pause; another knock; another pause; then the visitor retreated. When Alfred relit the candles he was looking smug. 'I know what *that* was. A boy I don't want to see any more.'

That led to talk of his unhappiness. Arthur, the most serious and long-lasting of all his loves, had left him. He was trying to force himself into an austere acceptance of solitude, but like a fool kept on hoping, kept on falling into situations which ended in disappointment, or worse. The boy on the stairs was the latest disappointment, a chance pick-up who turned out to be inadequate. I said: 'But Alfred, dear heart, what makes you think it *likely* that someone you pick up in a urinal will instantly turn into your own true love?'; to which he replied condescendingly that I had no sense of romance.

My two favourite memories of New York were given me by Alfred during my visit: he showed me the only pleasure in the city

which could still be had for a nickel, and he took me to Coney
Island. The nickel pleasure was riding the Staten Island ferry there
and back on a single fare, which meant hiding instead of landing at
the end of the outward journey. Early on a summer evening, when
the watery light and the ting-tong of a bell on a marker-buoy
almost turned Manhattan into Venice, it was indeed a charming
thing to do. And Coney Island was beautiful too, the water sleepy as
it lapped the dun-coloured sand, the sound of the boardwalk
underfoot evoking past summers which seemed – mysteriously – to
have been experienced by me. Sitting on the beach, we watched the
white flower of the parachute jump opening and floating down,
opening and floating down . . . Alfred teased me to make the jump
but I'm a coward about fairground thrills, and jibbed. He was
afraid, too, and told stories about famous accidents. He showed me
where, when he was a child, he used to climb down into the secret
runways under the boardwalk, and instructed me in methods of
cheating so that this or that could be seen or done without paying.
He was fond and proud of the child who used to play truant there
and had become so expert at exploiting the place's delights, and as
we sat beside each other in the subway, going home, I felt more
comfortably accepted by New York than I had ever done before. I
don't remember him ever talking about the pleasures of being an
enfant terrible reviewer, capable of causing a considerable frisson in
literary New York, which he was at that time.

Being the publisher of someone whose books are good but don't
sell is an uncomfortable business. Partly you feel guilt (did we miss
chances? Could we have done this or that more effectively?), and
partly irritation (does he really expect us to disregard all commercial considerations for the sake of his book?). Alfred gained a

reputation for persecuting his publishers and agents with irrational demands, but with us he was never more than tetchy, and most of the uneasiness I felt came from my own disappointment rather than from his bullying. In England he was all but overlooked: a few reviewers made perfunctory acknowledgement of his cleverness and the unusual nature of his imagination, but many more failed to mention him. Our fiction list was well thought of by literary editors, and I had written them personal letters about Alfred. I was driven to wondering whether the favour we were in had backfired: had they – or some of them – taken against his work and decided that it would be kinder to us not to review it at all, rather than to review it badly? Only John Davenport, a good critic who had become Alfred's friend out of admiration for his writing, spoke out with perceptive enthusiasm.

I have forgotten when Alfred moved to Morocco and whether he told me why he was doing so (Paul Bowles had suggested it at a party in New York). The first letter that I still have with a Tangier address was written soon after the publication in England of his collection of stories, *Behold Goliath*, early in 1965.

Dear Rat

Why haven't you written?

Why didn't you let me know about publication?

Why haven't you sent me copies?

Why haven't you sent me reviews?

I will not make you suffer by asking why you didn't use the Burroughs quote, though I would like you to volunteer an explanation. I hope you will write me by return of post.

I'm coming to England, either driving in my trusty little Austin or by plane which terrifies me. I'm coming with my

Moroccan boyfriend, and the real reason for the trip is to get his foot operated on. He has a spur, an excrescence of bone on the left heel, due to a rheumatic process. I'm afraid of doctors here. But please keep this a secret as they probably won't let us into England if they find out . . . I would appreciate it if you would check up on surgeons, bone surgeons or orthopedic specialists. I have some money so it doesn't have to be the health insurance thing, though that would help . . . They always used to fuss about me at the frontier, so there's bound to be a fuss about Dris. I am going to tell them that we are going to be your guests over the summer. I hope this is okay with you (for me to say so, not for us to stay) and that if they phone you or anything you will say yes it's true. Please reply at once.

Oh, I don't know if Norman [Glass] mentioned it, but I don't wear a wig any more. I thought I'd better tell you in advance so you don't go into shock. I like it better this way, but I'm still somewhat self-conscious.

Edward [Field] says I must give you and Monique Nathan* a copy of *The Exquisite Corpse* immediately. Epstein** says: 'I doubt very much that I can publish the book in a way that will be satisfactory to you, and I don't want to compound our joint disappointment in *Goliath*. The other reason has to do with the book itself. I recognize its brilliance – or more accurately I recognize your brilliance – but I confess that I'm baffled by your intentions, and I'm concerned that I would not know how to present

---

* His editor at Editions du Seuil, Paris
** His editor at Random House, New York

the book effectively. I don't mean that for me the book didn't work; simply that it worked in ways I only partly understood. Or in ways that suggest it is more a poem than a novel, though whether this distinction clarifies anything is a puzzle.'

The book is too simple for him. It reads like a children's book and requires innocence of a reader. Imagine asking Jason Epstein to be innocent ...

Will let you see it when I come. PLEASE REPLY BY RETURN OF POST. Love.

My answer:

I did tell you publication date, I have sent you copies – or rather, copies were sent, as is customary, to your agent (if A. M. Heath is still your agent – they are on paper. I called them this morning and they said they'd post your six copies today, and I don't know why they haven't done this before). Here are copies of the main reviews [my lack of comment makes their disappointing nature evident]. And I didn't put the Burroughs quote on the jacket because no one in Sales wanted me to, Burroughs being thought of here except by the few as dangerously far out and obscene, and they not wanting to present you as more for the few than you are. Should have told you this. Sorry.

I am enclosing a letter of invitation in case it may be useful with the visa people or at frontiers. It's marvellous that you are coming ...

Your quote from Jason Epstein made me laugh – there's a nervous publisher backing against a wall if ever there was

one. I was also, of course, scared by his reaction because
there is nothing more twitch-inducing than waiting for
something to come in which you know is going to be unlike
anything else, for fear that it is going to be so unlike that
one will have hideous forebodings about its fate. I'm dying
to read it. Hurrah hurrah that you'll soon be here. Love.

His answer, written in a mellow mood, ended with the words: 'As
for *The Exquisite Corpse* being unlike, yes, it is probably the most
unlike book you've read since childhood. And probably, also, the
most delicious.'

I could not have rejected *The Exquisite Corpse*, because it seemed –
still seems – to me to draw the reader into itself with irresistible
seductions. Alfred was right: you must read it as a child in that
you must read it simply for what happens next, without trying to
impose 'inner meanings' on it. The title comes from the game called
in England 'Consequences' – it was the Surrealists who gave it the
more exotic name. Do people still play it? A small group of people
take a sheet of paper, the first person writes the opening line of a
miniature story, then folds the paper so that the next person can't
see what he has written; the next person writes the next line, and
folds – and so on to the last person, whose line must start 'and the
consequence was . . .' Unfold the paper and you have a nonsense
story which is often delightfully bizarre. You can do it with drawing, as well as with words: I can still remember a sublime monster
produced that way by my cousins and me when I was a child, far
more astonishing than anything any of us could have thought up
on our own, yet perfectly convincing. Alfred followed the 'consequences' principle – it's as though the paper were folded between

each chapter, and when people you have already met reappear you are not always sure that they are the same people – perhaps the name has been given to someone else? Sometimes appalling or obscene things happen to them (I still find it hard to take the scene in which the character called Xavier watches his papa dying). Often it is monstrously funny. In no way is the writing 'difficult'. There is nothing experimental about the syntax; you are not expected to pick up veiled references or make subtle associations; and there can never be a moment's doubt about what is happening to the characters. The writing – so natural, so spontaneous-feeling, so precise – makes them, as Alfred claimed, delicious. The book's strangeness lies entirely in the events, as it does in a fairy-story, remote though Alfred's events are (and they could hardly be remoter) from those of Hans Andersen.

I was captivated, but two things disturbed me. The first was that we would be no more able than Jason Epstein to turn this extremely 'unlike' book into a best-seller, so Alfred was bound to be disappointed. And the second was that it left me feeling 'one inch madder, and it would have been too mad'.

This was something to do with the contrast between the perfection and airiness of the writing and the wildness of the events. The easy elegance, the wit, the sweet reason of the style are at the service of humour, yes; of inventiveness, yes; but also of something fierce and frightening. A fierce – an aggressive – despair? If aggressive despair is screamed and thumped at you it is painful, but it makes sense. When it is flipped at you lightly, almost playfully . . . Well, it doesn't make nonsense, because nothing so lucid could be called nonsensical, but (like Jason Epstein) I don't know for sure what it does make. I am captivated, but I am uneasy. I am uneasy, but I am captivated. The balance wobbles and comes to rest on the side of captivation. I use the present tense because I have just reread it for the first time in years, and reacted to it exactly as I did at the first reading.

When Alfred arrived with Dris he was wigless. He looked impressive, face, scalp, ears, neck all tanned evenly by the Moroccan sun. Although he himself had already broken the taboo, I still felt nervous and had to screw up my courage in order to congratulate him on his appearance. I don't think I am inventing the shyly happy expression on his face as he accepted the congratulations. As I learnt later, having to wear a wig because a childhood illness had left him hairless was the most terrible thing in his life, an affliction loaded almost beyond bearing with humiliation and rage; so throwing it off, which had taken great courage, was a vastly important event to him.

Morocco, I thought, had given him a new calm and freedom, and he agreed. The version he gave me of the place was all liberation and gentleness: you could smoke delicious kif there as naturally as English people drink tea; no strict line was drawn between hetero- and homosexual love; and you didn't have to wear a wig – you could be wholly yourself. I rejoiced for him that he had found the place he needed.

A couple of days later he brought Dris to dinner at my place: handsome, cheerful Dris, with whom I could communicate only by smiling because I have no Spanish. After dinner Alfred sent him into the kitchen to wash the dishes, which shocked me until they had both convinced me that it was dull for him to sit listening to incomprehensible English. Soon Dris stuck his head round the door and offered me his younger brother – he thought it wrong that I should have no one to do my housework. Alfred advised against it, saying that the boy was beautiful but a handful and that Dris constantly had to chivvy him out of louche bars. Dris himself had become a model of respectability now that he had a loving and reliable American, and Alfred – so he said – would one day be the guest of honour at Dris's wedding. That would be recognized in Morocco as the proper conclusion of their relationship, and probably Dris's wife would do Alfred's laundry while their children would be like family for him. It sounded idyllic.

The high point of the evening was the story of their adventures on their drive to England, told with parentheses in Spanish so that Dris could participate. Alfred had crashed the car in France. When the police came Dris was lying on the ground with blood on his head. It was really only a scratch but it looked much worse and Dris was groaning and rolling up his eyes so that only the whites were visible. Yes, yes, Dris intervened, sparkling with delight, with Alfred interpreting in his wake. He had suddenly remembered that a friend of his had been in an accident in France, and was taken to hospital, and when he got there he *was given all his meals for free*! So Dris decided in a flash to get to hospital where he would save Alfred money by getting fed, and also – this was the inspiration which filled him with glee – by complaining piteously about his foot, as though it had been hurt in the accident, he would make them X-ray his foot, as well as feed him, so that Alfred would not have to pay for an X-ray in London. Unfortunately this brilliant wheeze came to nothing because he was not allowed to smoke in the ward, so before he could be X-rayed he became too fed up to endure it, and walked out. It was pure luck, Alfred said, that they had run into each other as they wandered the streets.

Alfred's gloss to the story was that the police and ambulance men had been fussing around so that Dris had no chance to explain his plan. Alfred had seen him whisked away without knowing where to, and had spent a day and a night adrift, wondering how the hell he was going to find Dris – and, indeed, whether Dris was still alive. Later this struck me as odd. It is not difficult to ask a policeman where an ambulance is going, nor to find a hospital. I supposed he must have been stoned out of his mind at the time of the accident, although I had never seen him more than mildly high and he was always careful to give me the impression that mildly high was as far as he went. I sometimes thought that Alfred tended to see me as slightly Jane-Austenish, which caused him to keep his less Jane-Austenish side averted from my view.

I didn't see much of him on that visit. He was affectionate and easy, but after a couple of hours I would know that I was becoming an inhibiting presence, and assume that he wanted to bring out the kif – I was unaware, then, that he also used other drugs – which I didn't use, so I would say goodnight and leave, feeling that the real evening was starting up behind me. Dris's foot remained a mystery. He saw a doctor, he did not have an operation, someone told me that the spur had been diagnosed as a result of gonorrhoea; and Alfred, when questioned, was vague, as though the matter had become unimportant.

Alfred's next visit, two years later, came out of the blue. As I came into the office one morning the receptionist behind her keyboard half rose from her chair and signalled that someone was waiting to see me. I peeked round the corner, and there was Alfred, sitting in a hunched position, staring into space. 'Oh my God, trouble' . . . the reaction was instantaneous, although his attitude might, I suppose, have been attributed to weariness.

I welcomed him and took him to my room, asking the usual

questions and getting the information that he was on his way back to Morocco from New York and had stopped off because he needed to see a dentist. Would I find him one, and would I give him some typing to do so that he could earn a little money while he was here? Of course I would. And then, in a tone which indicated that this was the visit's real purpose: 'Will you call the Prime Minister and tell him to stop it.'

Stop what?

The voices.

I must not attempt dialogue or I will start cheating. The voices had been driving him mad. They gave him no peace, and the most dreadful thing about them was that they, not he, had written every word of his work. Did I see how appalling it was: learning that he had *never* existed? And even Dris was on their side. They often came at night, very loud. Jeering at him. Dris, in bed beside him, *must* have heard them. He could only be lying when he insisted that he didn't. It was not really for the money that Alfred needed the typing, it was because it might drown the voices.

He had been to New York, where he had attacked his mother with a knife (he had attacked Dris, too; though whether it was at this point, or a little later, that I learnt about these attacks I cannot remember). He was in London now because of what I had told him in Fez. But I had never been to Fez. Oh yes, I had, last week. Alarm became more specific because of the stony way he looked at me: I saw that it was possible to become one of 'them', an enemy, at any moment. I said cautiously that this Fez business puzzled me, because certainly my *physical* self had been in London last week.

I told him I had never met the Prime Minister (Harold Wilson it was then), and would not be put through to him if I called him, but that I could approach a Member of Parliament if that would do. I also told him that I was sure the voices were a delusion. He replied that he could understand my disbelief, and that I thought he was mad, so could I not in return understand that to him the voices were real: 'As real as a bus going down the street'? Yes, I could grant that, which seemed to help. It enabled him to make a bargain with me. If I proved that I was taking him seriously by approaching an MP, he would take me seriously enough to see a doctor.

That settled, things began to go with astonishing slickness. When I called my dentist I got through in seconds and he was able to see Alfred that afternoon; and it turned out that we had in the office a manuscript which genuinely needed to be retyped. Both these pieces of luck seemed providential, because I was sure that Alfred would have interpreted delay or difficulty as obstruction. (He kept all his appointments with the dentist, behaving normally while there, and he typed the manuscript faultlessly.)

After he had gone I sat there shaking: it would not have been very much more of a shock if I had come across someone dead. Then I pulled myself together and went to discuss the crisis with the person in the office most likely to know something about madness, who recommended calling the Tavistock Clinic for advice. At that time Doctors Laing and Cooper were in their heyday, and someone at the clinic suggested that I should get in touch with Laing. He was away, so his secretary passed me on to Cooper.

Dr Cooper agreed to see Alfred, told me that having offered to speak to an MP I must do so – it would be a bad mistake to cheat – and asked me who would be paying him. Alfred's family, I extemporized, hoping devoutly that it would not end by being me; and when, next day, I managed to speak to Alfred's brother in New York, he agreed. He sounded agitated, but a good deal nicer than Alfred's rare references to him had suggested. Then I called an MP of my acquaintance who said: 'Are you out of *your* mind? If you knew the number of nuts we get, asking us to stop the voices . . .'

The thought of telling Alfred that afternoon that the MP would not play worried me enough for me to ask someone to stay within earshot of my room while he was with me. To my surprise he took the news calmly, and agreed to visit Dr Cooper in spite of my failure. I began to see what I had been doing, talking to him in Fez: of all his friends I was probably the one most likely to think of madness in terms of illness, and of illness in terms of seeing a doctor, and because we saw little of each other I had not yet turned into an enemy. Alfred *wanted* to be proved wrong about the voices, he *wanted* someone to force him into treatment. I had been chosen as the person most likely to do that.

Nevertheless he could bring himself to visit Dr Cooper only once, because: 'I don't like him, he looks like an Irish bookmaker.' Cooper then volunteered to find a psychiatric social worker to talk him through this crisis, telling me that if this one could be overcome, Alfred would be less likely to experience another – perhaps. A pleasant, eager young man came to me for a briefing, then started to make regular visits to Alfred who had found himself a room in a remote suburb – I think it was lent to him by friends, but I didn't know them. What Alfred thought of his conversations with the psychiatric social worker I never heard, but the young man told me that he felt privileged to be in communication with such a mind. I remember fearing that Alfred would draw the young man into his world before the young man could draw him back into ours.

Two, or perhaps three weeks went by, during which I called Alfred a couple of times – he sounded lifeless – but did not ask him to my place or visit him at his. I knew I ought to do so, but kept putting it off. This was my first experience of mental illness, and I felt without bearings in strange and dangerous territory. Having taken such practical steps as I was able to think of, I found to my shame that the mere thought of Alfred exhausted me and that my affection was not strong enough to overcome the exhaustion. Not yet ... next week, perhaps ... until the telephone rang and it was the psychiatric social worker reporting that Alfred had left for Morocco – and I felt a wave of guilty relief. Asked whether he was better, the young man sounded dubious: 'He was able to make the decision, anyway.' And after that I never heard from Alfred again.

I suppose it was his New York agent who sent me a copy of 'The Foot', his last novel, which has never been published. There was wonderful stuff in it, particularly about his childhood and losing his hair – when the wig was first put on his head, he wrote, it was as though his skull had been split with an axe ... But much of the book had gone over the edge into the time of the voices. After reading 'The Foot' I saw why *The Exquisite Corpse* is so extraordinarily vivid: more than anyone had realized at the time, its strange events had been as real to Alfred 'as a bus going down the street'. He was already entering the dislocated reality of madness, but was still able to keep his hold on style: instead of leaving the reader, flustered, on the edge of that reality, he could carry us into it. When he came to write 'The Foot' his style had started to slither out of his grasp. By that time the sickness which found such nourishment in the 'liberation and gentleness' of Morocco, with its abundance of delicious kif, had won.

Without knowing it, Alfred left me a delightful legacy: his oldest and truest friend, the poet Edward Field. Some years ago Edward's tireless campaign to revive Alfred's reputation in the United States caused him to get in touch with me, and almost instantly he and his friend, the novelist Neil Derrick, took their place among my most treasured friends. It is Edward who told me about Alfred's last, sad years.

Back in Morocco, his behaviour became so eccentric that he lost all his friends and alarmed the authorities. He was thrown out, and moved with his dogs – new ones, not Columbine and Skoura – to Israel, where he survived by becoming almost a hermit, still tormented by the voices and trying frantically to drown them with drink and drugs. I was shown by Edward what was probably the last thing he ever wrote: a piece intended to be published in a periodical as 'A Letter from Israel'. It was heart-breaking. Gone was the sparkle, gone the vitality, humour and imagination. All it contained was baffled misery at his own loneliness and hopelessness. The madness, having won, had turned his writing – a bitter paradox – far more *ordinary* than it had ever been before. The world he was describing was no longer magical (magical in horror as well as in beauty), but was drab, cruel, boring – 'mad' only in that the mundane and tedious persecutions to which he constantly believed himself subject were, to other people, obviously of his own making. When he died – probably from heart failure brought on by drugs and alcohol – he was alone in a rented house which he hated. It is true that his death cannot be regretted, but feeling like that about the death of dear, amazing Alfred is horribly sad. However, other people are now joining Edward in keeping his writing alive in the United States: it is still a small movement, but it is a real one. May it thrive!

V. S. NAIPAUL

GOOD PUBLISHERS ARE supposed to 'discover' writers, and perhaps they do. To me, however, they just happened to come.
V. S. Naipaul came through Andrew Salkey who was working with
him at the BBC, and Andrew I met through Mordecai Richler when
he took me for a drink in a Soho club. When Andrew heard that I
was Mordecai's editor he asked me if he could send me a young
friend of his who had just written something very good, and a few
days later Vidia came to a coffee bar near our office and handed me
Miguel Street.

I was delighted by it, but worried: it was stories (though linked
stories), and a publishing dogma to which André Deutsch strongly
adhered was that stories didn't sell unless they were by Names. So
before talking to him about it I gave it to Francis Wyndham who
was with us as part-time 'Literary Adviser', and Francis loved it at
once and warmly. This probably tipped the balance with André,
whose instinct was to distrust as 'do-gooding' my enthusiasm for a
little book by a West Indian about a place which interested no one

and where the people spoke an unfamiliar dialect. I think he welcomed its being stories because it gave him a reason for saying 'no': but Francis's opinion joined to mine made him bid me find out if the author had a novel on the stocks and tell him that if he had, then that should come first and the stories could follow all in good time. Luckily Vidia was in the process of writing *The Mystic Masseur*.

In fact we could well have launched him with *Miguel Street*, which has outlasted his first two novels in critical esteem, because in the fifties it was easier to get reviews for a writer seen by the British as black than it was for a young white writer, and reviews influenced readers a good deal more then than they do now. Publishers and reviewers were aware that new voices were speaking up in the newly independent colonies, and partly out of genuine interest, partly out of an optimistic if ill-advised sense that a vast market for books lay out there, ripe for development, they felt it to be the thing to encourage those voices. This trend did not last long, but it served to establish a number of good writers.

Vidia did not yet have the confidence to walk away from our shilly-shallying, and fortunately it did him no real harm. Neither he nor we made any money to speak of from his first three books, *The Mystic Masseur*, *The Suffrage of Elvira* and *Miguel Street*, but there was never any doubt about the making of his name, which began at once with the reviews and was given substance by his own work as a reviewer, of which he got plenty as soon as he became known as a novelist. He was a very good reviewer, clearly as widely read as any literary critic of the day, and it was this rather than his first books which revealed that here was a writer who was going to reject the adjective 'regional', and with good reason.

We began to meet fairly often, and I enjoyed his company

because he talked well about writing and people, and was often funny. At quite an early meeting he said gravely that when he was up at Oxford – which he had not liked – he once did a thing so terrible that he would never be able to tell anyone what it was. I said it was unforgivable to reveal that much without revealing more, especially to someone like me who didn't consider even murder literally unspeakable, but I couldn't shift him and never learnt what the horror was – though someone told me later that when he was at Oxford Vidia did have some kind of nervous breakdown. It distressed me that he had been unhappy at a place which I loved. Having such a feeling for scholarship, high standards and tradition he ought to have liked it . . . but no, he would not budge. Never for a minute did it occur to me that he might have felt at a loss when he got to Oxford because of how different it was from his background, still less because of any form of racial insult: he appeared to me far too impressive a person to be subject to such discomforts.

The image Vidia was projecting at that time, in his need to protect his pride, was so convincing that even when I read *A House for Mr Biswas* four years later, and was struck by the authority of his account of Mr Biswas's nervous collapse, I failed to connect its painful vividness with his own reported 'nervous breakdown'. Between me and the truth of his Oxford experience stood the man he wanted people to see.

At that stage I did not know how or why he had rejected Trinidad, and if I had known it, would still have been unable to understand what it is like to be unable to accept the country in which you were born. Vidia's books (not least *A Way in the World*, not written until thirty-seven years later) were to do much to educate me; but then I had no conception of how someone who feels he doesn't belong to his 'home' and cannot belong anywhere else is forced to exist only in himself; nor of how exhausting and precarious such a condition (blithely seen by the young and ignorant as desirable) can be. Vidia's self – his very being – was his writing: a great gift, but all he had. He was to report that ten years later in his career, when he had earned what seemed to others an obvious security, he was still tormented by anxiety about finding the matter for his next book, and for the one after that . . . an anxiety not merely about earning his living, but about *existing as the person he wanted to be*. No wonder that while he was still finding his way into his writing he was in danger; and how extraordinary that he could nevertheless strike an outsider as a solidly impressive man*.

This does not mean that I failed to see the obvious delicacy of his nervous system. Because of it I was often worried by his lack of money, and was appalled on his behalf when I once saw him risk losing a commission by defying *The Times Literary Supplement*. They had offered their usual fee of £25 (or was it guineas?) for a review, and he had replied haughtily that he wrote nothing for less than fifty. 'Oh silly Vidia,' I thought, 'now they'll never offer him anything again.' But lo! they paid him his fifty and I was filled with admiration. Of course he was right: authors ought to know their own value and refuse the insult of derisory fees.

I was right to admire that self-respect, at that time, but it was going to develop into a quality difficult to like. In all moral qualities the line between the desirable and the deplorable is imprecise – between tolerance and lack of discrimination, prudence and cowardice, generosity and extravagance – so it is not easy to see where

---

* Since writing this I have read the letters which Vidia and his father exchanged while Vidia was at Oxford. *Letters Between a Father and Son* fully reveals the son's loneliness and misery, and makes the self he was able to present to the world even more extraordinary.

a man's proper sense of his own worth turns into a more or less pompous self-importance. In retrospect it seems to me that it took eight or nine years for this process to begin to show itself in Vidia, and I think it possible that his audience was at least partly to blame for it.

For example, after a year or so of meetings in the pubs or restaurants where I usually lunched, I began to notice that Vidia was sometimes miffed at being taken to a cheap restaurant or being offered a cheap bottle of wine – and the only consequence of my seeing this (apart from my secretly finding it funny) was that I became careful to let him choose both restaurant and wine. And this carefulness not to offend him, which was, I think, shared by all, or almost all, his English friends, came from an assumption that the reason why he was so anxious to command respect was fear that it was, or might be, denied him because of his race; which led to a squeamish dismay in oneself at the idea of being seen as racist. The shape of an attitude which someone detests, and has worked at extirpating, can often be discerned from its absence, and during the first years of Vidia's career in England he was often coddled for precisely the reason the coddler was determined to disregard.

Later, of course, the situation changed. His friends became too used to him to see him as anything but himself, and those who didn't know him saw him simply as a famous writer – on top of which he could frighten people. Then it was the weight and edge of his personality which made people defer to him, rather than consideration for his sensitivity. Which makes it easy to underestimate the pain and strain endured by that sensitivity when he had first pulled himself up out of the thin, sour soil in which he was reared, and was striving to find a purchase in England where, however warmly he was welcomed, he could never feel that he wholly belonged.

During the sixties I visited the newly independent islands of Trinidad & Tobago twice, with intense pleasure: the loveliness of tropical forests and seas, the jolt of excitement which comes from *difference*, the kindness of people, the amazing beauty of Carnival (unlike Vidia, I like steel bands: oh the sound of them coming in from the fringes of Port of Spain through the four-o'clock-in-the-morning darkness of the opening day!). On my last morning in Port of Spain I felt a sharp pang as I listened to the keskidee (a bird which really does seem to say *'Qu'est-ce qu'il dit?'*) and knew how unlikely it was that I should ever hear it again. But at no time was it difficult to remember that mine was a visitor's Trinidad & Tobago; so three other memories, one from high on the country's social scale, the others from lower although by no means from the bottom, are just as clear as the ones I love.

One. Vidia's history of the country, *The Loss of El Dorado*, which is rarely mentioned nowadays but which I think is the best of his non-fiction books, had just come out. Everyone I had met, including the Prime Minister Eric Williams and the poet Derek Walcott, had talked about it in a disparaging way and had betrayed as they did so that they had not read it. At last, at a party given by the leader of the opposition, I met someone who had: an elderly Englishman just retiring from running the Coast Guard. We were both delighted to be able to share our pleasure in it and had a long talk about it. As we parted I asked him: 'Can you really be the only person in this country who has read it?' and he answered sadly: 'Oh, easily.'

Two. In Tobago I stayed in a delightful little hotel where on most evenings the village elders dropped in for a drink. On one of them a younger man – a customs officer in his mid-thirties seconded to Tobago's chief town Scarborough, from Port of Spain – invited me to go out on the town with him. We were joined by another customs officer and a nurse from the hospital. First we went up to Scarborough's fort – its Historic Sight – to look at the view. Then, when conversation fizzled out, it was suggested that we should have a drink at the Arts Centre. It looked in the darkness little more than a shed, and it was shut, but a man was hunted up who produced the key, some Coca-Cola and half a bottle of rum . . . and there we stood, under a forty-watt lamp in a room of utter dinginess which contained nothing at all but a dusty ping-pong table with a very old copy of the *Reader's Digest* lying in the middle of it. We sipped our drinks in an atmosphere of embarrassment – almost shame – so heavy that it silenced us. After a few minutes we gave up and went to my host's barely furnished but tidy little flat – I remember it as cold, which it can't have been – where we listened to a record of 'Yellow Bird' and drank another rum. Then I was driven back to the hotel. The evening's emptiness – the really frightening feeling of nothing to do, nothing to say – had made me feel quite ill. I knew too little about the people I had been with to guess what they were like when at ease: all I could discern was that my host was bored to distraction at having to work in the sticks; that he had been driven by his boredom to make his sociable gesture and had then become nervous to the extent of summoning friends to his aid; and that all three had quickly seen that the whole thing was a mistake and had been overtaken by embarrassed gloom. And no wonder. When I remember the Arts Centre I see why, when Vidia first revisited the West Indies, what he felt was fear.

Three. And it is not only people like Vidia, feverish with

repressed talent, who yearn to escape. There was the conversation
I overheard in the changing-cubicle next to mine when I was trying
on a swimsuit in a store in Port of Spain. An American woman,
accompanied by her husband, was also buying something, and they
were obviously quite taken by the pretty young woman who was
serving them. They were asking her questions about her family, and
the heightened warmth of their manner made me suspect that they
found it almost exciting to be kind to a black person. When the cus-
tomer had made her choice and her husband was writing a cheque,
the saleswoman's voice suddenly changed from chirpiness to
breathlessness and she said: 'May I ask you something?' The wife
said: 'Yes, of course,' and the poor young woman plunged into desperate pleading: please, please would they help her, would they
give her a letter inviting her to their home which she could show to
the people who issued visas, she wouldn't be any trouble, and if
they would do this for her . . . On and on she went, the husband
trying to interrupt her in an acutely embarrassed voice, still wanting to sound kind but only too obviously appalled at what his
entirely superficial amiability had unleashed. Soon the girl was in
tears and the couple were sounding frantic with remorse and anxiety to escape – and I was so horrified at being the invisible and
unwilling witness of this desperate young woman's humiliation
that I abandoned my swimsuit, scrambled into my dress and fled,
so I do not know how it ended.

Vidia had felt fear and dislike of Trinidad ever since he could
remember. As a schoolboy he had written a vow on an endpaper of
his Latin primer to be gone within five years (it took him six). He
remembered this in *The Middle Passage*, his first non-fiction book,
published in 1962, in which he described his first revisiting of the

West Indies and did something he had never done before: examined the reasons why he feared and hated the place where he was born.

It was a desperately negative view of the place, disregarding a good half of the picture; and it came out with the fluency and force of something long matured less in the mind than in the depths of the nervous system. Trinidad, he said, was and knew itself to be a mere dot on the map. It had no importance and no existence as a nation, being only somewhere out of which first Spain, then France, then Britain could make money: grossly easy money because of using slaves to do the work, and after slaves indentured labour which was almost as cheap. A slave-based society has no need to be efficient, so no tradition of efficiency exists. Slave-masters don't need to be intelligent, so 'in Trinidad education was not one of the things money could buy; it was something money freed you from. Education was strictly for the poor. The white boy left school "counting on his fingers" as the Trinidadian likes to say, but this was a measure of his privilege . . . The white community was never an upper class in the sense that it possessed superior speech or taste or attainments; it was envied only for its money and its access to pleasure.'

When this crude colonial society was opened up because the islands were no longer profitable and the British pulled out, what Vidia saw gushing in to fill the vacuum was the flashiest and most materialistic kind of American influence in the form of commercial radio (television had yet to come) and films – films at their most violent and unreal. ('British films', he wrote, 'played to empty houses. It was my French master who urged me to go to see *Brief Encounter*; and there were two of us in the cinema, he in the balcony, I in the pit.') Trinidad & Tobago was united only in its hunger for 'American modernity', and under that sleazy veneer it was split.

It was split between the descendants of slaves, the African Trinidadians, and the descendants of indentured labourers, the Indians; both groups there by an accident of history, neither with any roots to speak of. In *The Middle Passage* Vidia called the Africans 'Negroes', which today sounds shocking. Reading the book one has to keep reminding oneself that the concept of Black Power had yet to be formulated. Black people had not yet rejected the word 'Negro': it was still widely used and 'black' was considered insulting. And in this book his main criticism of Trinidadians of African descent is that they had been brainwashed by the experience of slavery into 'thinking white' – into being ashamed of their own colour and physical features. What he deplored – as many observers of West Indian societies had done – was precisely the attitudes which people of African descent were themselves beginning to deplore, and would soon be forcing themselves to overcome.

The Indians he saw as less unsure of themselves because of the pride they took in the idea of India; but he also saw that idea as being almost meaningless – they had no notion of what the sub-continent was really like. It was also dangerous in that it militated against attempts to bridge the rift. The Indians were 'a peasant-minded, money-minded community, spiritually static, its religion reduced to rites without philosophy, set in a materialist, colonialist society; a combination of historical accident and national temperament has turned the Trinidadian Indian into the complete colonial, even more philistine than the white.'

He sums up his account of racial friction thus: 'Like monkeys pleading for evolution, each claiming to be whiter than the other, Indians and Negroes appeal to the unacknowledged white audience to see how much they despise one another. They despise one another by reference to the whites; and the irony is that their antagonism should have reached its peak today, when white prejudices have ceased to matter.'

This was a fair assessment: everyone, apart from Tourist Board propagandists, to whom I talked about politics deplored this racial tension, and most of them either said outright, or implied, that blame lay with the group to which they did not belong. No one remarked on the common sense which enabled people to rub along in spite of it (as they still do), any more than Vidia did. The rift, which certainly was absurd and regrettable, became more dramatic if seen as dangerous, and therefore reflected a more lurid light on whoever was being presented as its instigator. People did make a bid for the outsider's respect – did 'appeal to the unacknowledged white audience'. But to what audience was Vidia himself appealing? It was *The Middle Passage* which first made black West Indians call him 'racist'.

The book was admired in England and disliked in Trinidad, but it was not addressed to the white audience in order to please it. Its whole point was to show that Caribbean societies are a mess because they were callously created by white men for the white men's own ends, only to be callously administered and finally callously abandoned. Vidia was trying to write from a point of view above that of white or brown or black; he was trying to look at the people now inhabiting the West Indies with a clear-sighted and impartial intelligence, and to describe what he saw honestly, even if honesty seemed brutal. This he felt, and said, had to be done because a damaged society shuffling along with the help of fantasies and excuses can only become more sick: what it has to do is learn to know itself, and only its writers can teach it that. Caribbean writers had so far, he claimed, failed to do more than plead their own causes. If he expected Trinidadians to welcome this high-minded message he was naive – but I don't suppose he did. He was pursuing his own understanding of the place, and offering it, because that is what a serious writer can't help doing. If anyone resented it, too bad.

Of course they did resent it – who doesn't resent hearing disagreeable truths told in a manner verging on the arrogant? But I think the label 'racist' which they stuck on him was, so to speak, only a local one. I saw him as a man raised in, and frightened by, a somewhat disorderly, inefficient and self-deceiving society, who therefore longed for order, clarity and competence. Having concluded that the lack of these qualities in the place where he was born came from the people's lack of roots, he over-valued a sense of history and respect for tradition, choosing to romanticize their results rather than to see the complex and far from admirable scenes with which they often co-exist. (His first visit to India, described in *An Area of Darkness*, left him in a state of distress because it showed him that an ancient civilization in which he had dared to hope that he would find the belonging he hungered for could be just as disorderly and inefficient as the place where he was born.) Although both England and the United States were each in its own way going to fall short of his ideal society, Europe as a whole came more close, more often, to offering a life in which he could feel comfortable. I remember driving, years ago, through a vine-growing region of France and coming on a delightful example of an ancient expertise taking pleasure in itself: a particularly well cultivated vineyard which had a pillar rose – a deep pink pillar rose – planted as an exquisite punctuation at the end of every row.

Instantly – although it was weeks since I had seen or thought of him – he popped into my head: 'How Vidia would like that!'

But although I cannot see Vidia as racist in the sense of wanting to be white or to propitiate whites, I do think it is impossible to spend the first eighteen years of your life in a given set of circumstances without being shaped by them: and Vidia spent the first eighteen years of his life as a Trinidadian Indian*. Passionate though his determination to escape the limitations imposed by this fate was, and near though it came to achieving the impossible, it could not wholly free him from his conditioning.

In Chapter One of *The Middle Passage*, when he has only just boarded the boat-train which will take him to Southampton, there begins the following description. Into the corridor, out of the compartment next to Vidia's, had stepped 'a very tall and ill-made Negro. The disproportionate length of his thighs was revealed by his baggy trousers. His shoulders were broad and so unnaturally square that they seemed hunched and gave him an appearance of fragility. His light grey jacket was as long and loose as a short topcoat; his yellow shirt was dirty and the frayed collar undone; his tie was slack and askew. He went to the window, opened the ventilation gap, pushed his face through, turned slightly to his left, and spat. His face was grotesque. It seemed to have been smashed in from one cheek. One eye had narrowed; the thick lips had bunched into a circular swollen protuberance; the enormous nose was twisted. When, slowly, he opened his mouth to spit, his face became even more distorted. He spat in slow, intermittent dribbles.'

---

* Only one of his father's letters refers to anyone of African descent – and that one letter is frantically agitated: a niece has started to date a man half-Indian, half-African; how should he deal with this frightful event?

Vidia makes a slight attempt to give this man a role in the story of his journey by saying that he began to imagine that the poor creature was aware of him in a malign way, that at one moment their eyes met, that in the buffet car there he was again . . . but in fact once he has been described the man has no part to play, he is done with; in spite of which Vidia could not resist placing him right at the start of the book and *describing him in greater physical detail than anyone else in all its 232 pages.* I am not saying that this man was invented or that he may have been less dreadfully unattractive than we are told he was; but by choosing to pick him out and to *fix* on him, Vidia has given an indelible impression less of the man than of his own reaction: the dismayed recoil of a fastidious Trinidadian Indian from what he sees as an inferior kind of person. And I believe that if I were black I should from time to time, throughout his work, pick up other traces of this flinching presence hidden in the shadow behind one of the best English-language novelists we have. And even as part of the white audience I cannot help noticing the occasional touch of self-importance (increasing with the years) which I suspect to have its roots far back in the Trinidadian Indian's nervous defiance of disrespect.

Vidia's mother, handsome and benignly matronly, welcomed his publishers very kindly when they visited Trinidad, and gave the impression of being the beloved linchpin of her family. When I first met them, long before they had been stricken by the close-together deaths of one of the daughters and of Shiva, Vidia's younger and only brother, they impressed me as a flourishing lot: good-looking, intelligent, charming, successful. A married daughter told me that Mrs Naipaul 'divides her time between the Temple and the quarry' – the latter being a business belonging to her side

of the family, in which she was a partner. That she was not simply
a comfortable mother-figure became apparent when she told me
that she had just got home from attending a seminar on welding
and was very glad that she hadn't missed it because she had learnt
enough at it to be able to cut the number of welders they employed
at the quarry by half. Soon afterwards she threw more light on her
own character by making a little speech to me, after noticing my
surprise when she had appeared to be indifferent to some news
about Vidia. She had been, she said, a well-brought-up Hindu girl
of her generation, so she had been given no education and was
expected to obey her parents in everything, and that was what she
did. Then she was married ('And there was no nonsense about
falling in love in those days'), whereupon it was her husband she
had to obey in everything, and that was what she did. Then she had
her children, so of course it was her job to devote herself entirely to
them and bring them up as well as possible, and that was what she
did ('and I think I can say I made a good job of it'). 'But then I said
to myself, when I am fifty – FINISH. I will begin to live for myself.
And that is what I am doing now and they must get on with their
own lives.'

It was an impressive little thumbnail autobiography, but it left
questions in my mind. I had, after all, read *A House for Mr Biswas*,
the novel Vidia had based on his father's life, and had gained a
vivid picture of how humiliated Mr Biswas had been after his marriage into the much richer and more influential Tulsi family –
although I don't think I knew at that stage that Seepersad Naipaul,
Vidia's father, had once had a mental breakdown and had vanished
from his home for months. Clearly this attractive and – I was now
beginning to think – slightly formidable woman was greatly over-
simplifying her story, but I liked her; as I told Vidia when, soon

after this, he asked me if I did. 'Yes, very much,' I said; to which he replied: 'Everyone seems to. I hate her.'

I wish I had asked him what he meant by that. It was not the first time that I heard him, in a fit of irritation, strike out at someone with a fierce word, so I didn't think it was necessarily true (and anyway, dislike of a mother usually indicates damaged love). But uncertain though I remained about his feelings towards his mother, I knew that he loved his father, who had died soon after Vidia left Trinidad to come to Oxford. He wrote a moving introduction to the little volume of his father's stories which he gave us to publish in 1976, and he spoke about the way his father had introduced him to books. Seepersad Naipaul had possessed a remarkably strong and true instinct for writing which had overcome his cir- cumstances to the point of giving him a passion for such English classics as had come his way, and steering him into a writing job on the local newspaper. He had passed his passion on by reading aloud to Vidia and Kamla, the sister nearest to him, making the children stand up as he read to keep them from falling asleep – which seems to have impressed the importance of the ritual on them rather than to have put them off. Seepersad's own few stories were about Trinidadian village life, and the most important lesson he gave his son was 'Write about what you know', thus curing him of the young colonial's feeling that 'literature' had to be exotic – something belonging to the faraway world out of which came the books he found in the library. And I know of another piece of advice Seepersad gave his son which speaks for the truth of his instinct. Vidia had shown him a piece of would-be comic writing, and he told him not to strive for comedy but to let it arise naturally out of the story. It is sad to think of this man hobbled by the circum- stances of his life (see *A House for Mr Biswas*) and dying before he

could see his son break free. The mother was part of the 'circumstances' and the child sided with his father against her, of that I feel
sure.

I cannot remember how long it was – certainly several months,
perhaps even a year – before I learnt that Vidia was married. 'I have
found a new flat', he would say; 'I saw such-and-such a film last
week'; 'My landlady says': not once had he used the words 'we' or
'our'. I had taken it for granted that he lived in industrious loneliness,
which had seemed sad. So when at a party I glimpsed him at the far
end of a room with a young woman – an inconspicuously, even
mousily pretty young woman – and soon afterwards saw him leaving with her, I was pleased that he had found a girlfriend. The next
time he came to the office I asked who she was – and was astounded
when he answered, in a rather cross voice, 'My wife, of course.'

After that Pat was allowed to creep out of the shadows, but only
a little: and one day she said something that shocked me so much
that I know for certain that I am remembering it word-for-word. I
must have remarked on our not meeting earlier, and she replied:
'Vidia doesn't like me to come to parties because I'm such a bore.'

From that moment on, whenever I needed to cheer myself up by
counting my blessings, I used to tell myself 'At least I'm not married
to Vidia'.

It did not exactly turn me against him, I suppose because from
the beginning I had thought of him as an interesting person to
watch rather than as a friend. The flow of interest between us had
always been one-way – I can't remember ever telling him anything
about my own affairs, or wanting to – so this odd business of his
marriage was something extra to watch rather than something
repellent. Had he ever loved her – or did he still love her in some
twisted way? They had married while he was at Oxford: had he

done it out of loneliness, to enlarge the minuscule territory he could call his own now that he was out in the world? Or was it because she could keep him? She was working as a teacher and continued to do so well into their marriage. Or was it to shelter him from other women? He had once asked a man of my acquaintance: 'Do you know any *fast* women?', which my friend found funny (particularly as he was gay) but which seemed touching to me. As did Vidia's only attempt to make a pass at me. Pat was away and I had asked him to supper. Without warning he got to his feet, came across the room and tried to kiss me as I was coming through the door carrying a tray loaded with glasses. It hardly seemed necessary to put into words the rebuff which most of him was clearly anxious for, but to be on the safe side I did. Our friendship, I said gently, was too valuable to complicate in any way – and his face brightened with relief. That someone so lacking in sexual experience and so puritanical should have to resort to prostitutes (as he told *The New Yorker* in 1994, and as a passage in *The Mimic Men* suggests) is natural; though I guess he did so infrequently, and with distaste.

The little I saw of Vidia and Pat together was depressing: there was no sign of their enjoying each other, and the one whole weekend I spent with them they bickered ceaselessly, Pat's tetchiness as sharp as his (developed as a defence, I thought). When he was abroad she was scrupulously careful of his interests; she did research for him; sometimes he referred to showing her work in progress: he trusted her completely, and with reason, because he was evidently her *raison d'être*. And she made it unthinkable to speak critically of him in her presence. But always her talk was full of how tiresome it was for him that she was sick in aeroplanes, or fainted in crowds, or couldn't eat curries . . . and when I tried to introduce a subject other than him that would interest us both, such as West Indian politics or her work as a teacher, she never failed to run us aground yet again on some reference to her own inadequacy. At first I took it for granted that he had shattered her self-confidence, and I am still sure he did it no good. But later I suspected that there had always been something in her which accepted – perhaps even welcomed – being squashed.

In *A Way in the World*, writing (as usual) as though he were a single man, Vidia described himself as 'incomplete' in 'physical attractiveness, love, sexual fulfilment'. How terrible for a wife to be publicly wiped out in this way! Everyone who knew the Naipauls said how sorry they were for Pat, and I was sorry for her, too. But whatever Vidia's reason for marrying, he cannot have foreseen what their marriage, for whatever reason, was going to be like. He, too, probably deserved commiseration.

When his Argentinian friend Margaret first came to London he brought her to lunch with me. She was a lively, elegant woman who, though English by descent, was 'feminine' in the Latin-American style, sexy and teasing, with the appearance of having got him just where she wanted him. And he glowed with pride and pleasure. Afterwards he said he was thinking of leaving Pat, and when I was dismayed (could she exist without him?) said that the thought of giving up 'carnal pleasure' just when he'd discovered it was too painful to bear. Why not stay married and have an affair, I asked; which he appeared to think an unseemly suggestion, although it was what he then did for many years. What happened later I don't know, but in the early years of their relationship there was no sign of his squashing Margaret. He did, however, make one disconcerting remark. Did I not find it interesting, he asked, that there was so much cruelty in sex?

*

What began to wear me down in my dealings with Vidia (it was a long time before I allowed myself to acknowledge it) was his depression.

With every one of his books – and we published eighteen of them – there was a three-part pattern. First came a long period of peace while he was writing, during which we saw little of him and I would often have liked to see more, because I would be full of curiosity about the new book. Then, when it was delivered, there would be a short burst of euphoria during which we would have enjoyable meetings and my role would be to appreciate the work, to write the blurb, to hit on a jacket that pleased both him and us, and to see that the script was free of typist's errors (he was such a perfectionist that no editing, properly speaking, was necessary). Then came part three: post-publication gloom, during which his voice on the telephone would make my heart sink – just a little during the first few years, deeper and deeper with the passing of time. His voice became charged with tragedy, his face became haggard, his theme became the atrocious exhaustion and damage (the word *damage* always occurred) this book had inflicted on him, and all to what end? Reviewers were ignorant monkeys, publishers (this would be implied in a sinister fashion rather than said) were lazy and useless: what was the point of it all? Why did he go on?

It is natural that a writer who knows himself to be good and who is regularly confirmed in that opinion by critical comment should expect to become a best-seller, but every publisher knows that you don't necessarily become a best-seller by writing well. Of course you don't necessarily have to write badly to do it: it is true that some best-selling books are written astonishingly badly, and equally true that some are written very well. The quality of the writing – even the quality of the thinking – is irrelevant. It is a matter of whether or not a nerve is hit in the wider reading public as opposed to the serious one which is composed of people who are interested in writing as an art. Vidia has sold well in the latter, and has pushed a good way beyond its fringes by becoming famous – at a certain point many people in the wider reading public start to feel that they *ought* to read a writer – but it was always obvious that he was not going to make *big* money. An old friend of mine who reads a great deal once said to me apologetically: 'I'm sure he's very good, but I don't feel he's for me' – and she spoke for a large number of reading people.

Partly this is because of his subject matter, which is broadly speaking the consequences of imperialism: people whose countries once ruled empires relish that subject only if it is flavoured, however subtly, with nostalgia. Partly it is because he is not interested in writing about women, and when he does so usually does it with dislike: more women than men read novels. And partly it is because of his temperament. Once, when he was particularly low, we talked about surviving the horribleness of life and I said that I did it by relying on simple pleasures such as the taste of fruit, the delicious sensations of a hot bath or clean sheets, the way flowers tremble very slightly with life, the lilt of a bird's flight: if I were stripped of those pleasures . . . better not to imagine it! He asked if I could really depend on them and I said yes. I have a clear memory of the sad, puzzled voice in which he replied: 'You're very lucky, I can't.' And his books, especially his novels (after the humour which filled the first three drained away) are coloured – or perhaps I should say 'discoloured' – by this lack of what used to be called animal spirits. They impress, but they do not charm.

He was, therefore, displeased with the results of publication, which filled him always with despair, sometimes with anger as well. Once he descended on me like a thunderbolt to announce that he had just been into Foyles of Charing Cross Road and they didn't have a single copy of his latest book, published only two weeks earlier, in stock: not one! Reason told me this was impossible, but I have a lurking tendency to accept guilt if faced with accusation, and this tendency went into spasm: suppose the sales department really had made some unthinkable blunder? Well, if they had I was not going to face the ensuing mayhem single-handed, so I said: 'We must go and tell André at once.' Which we did; and André Deutsch said calmly: 'What nonsense, Vidia – come on, we'll go to Foyles straight away and I'll show you.' So all three of us stumped down the street to Foyles, only two minutes away, Vidia still thunderous, I twittering with nerves, André serene. Once we were in the shop he cornered the manager and explained: 'Mr Naipaul couldn't find his book: will you please show him where it is displayed.' – 'Certainly, Mr Deutsch': and there it was, two piles of six copies each, on the table for 'Recent Publications'. André said afterwards that Vidia looked even more thunderous at being done out of his grievance, but if he did I was too dizzy with relief to notice.

Vidia's anxiety and despair were real: you need only compare a photograph of his face in his twenties with one taken in his forties to see how it has been shaped by pain. It was my job to listen to his unhappiness and do what I could to ease it – which would not have been too bad if there had been anything I *could* do. But there was not: and exposure to someone else's depression is draining, even if only for an hour or so at a time and not very often. I felt genuinely sorry for him, but the routine was repeated so often . . . The truth is that as the years went by, during these post-publication glooms I had increasingly to force myself into feeling genuinely sorry for him, in order to endure him.

*

Self-brainwashing sometimes has to be a part of an editor's job. You are no use to the writers on your list if you cannot bring imaginative sympathy to working with them, and if you cease to be of use to them you cease to be of use to your firm. Imaginative sympathy cannot issue from a cold heart so you have to like your writers. Usually this is easy; but occasionally it happens that in spite of admiring someone's work you are – or gradually become – unable to like the person.

I thought so highly of Vidia's writing and felt his presence on our list to be so important that I simply could not allow myself not to like him. I was helped by a foundation of affection laid down during the early days of knowing him, and I was able to believe that his depressions hurt him far more than they hurt me – that he could not prevent them – that I ought to be better at bearing them than I was. And as I became more aware of other things that grated – his attitude to Pat and to his brother Shiva (whom he bullied like an enraged mother hen in charge of a particularly feckless chick) – I called upon a tactic often employed in families: Aunt Emily may have infuriating mannerisms or disconcerting habits, but they are forgiven, even enjoyed, because they are *so typically her*. The offending person is put into the position of a fictional, almost a cartoon, character, whose quirks can be laughed or marvelled at as though they existed only on a page. For quite a long time seeing him as a perpetrator of 'Vidia-isms' worked rather well.

In 1975 we received the thirteenth of his books – his eighth work of fiction – *Guerrillas*. For the first time I was slightly apprehensive because he had spoken to me about the experience of writing it in an unprecedented way: usually he kept the process private, but this time he said that it was extraordinary, something that had never happened before: it was as though the book had been *given* to him. Such a feeling about writing does not necessarily bode well. And as it turned out, I could not like the book.

It was about a Trinidad-like island sliding into a state of decadence, and there was a tinge of hysteria in the picture's dreadfulness, powerfully imagined though it was. A central part of the story came from something that had recently happened in Trinidad: the murder of an Englishwoman called Gail Benson who had changed her name to Halé Kimga, by a Trinidadian who called himself Michael X and who had set up a so-called 'commune'. Gail had been brought to Trinidad by her lover, a black American known as Hakim Jamal (she had changed her name at his bidding). Both of the men hovered between being mad and being con-men, and their linking-up had been Gail's undoing. I knew all three, Gail and Hakim well, Michael very slightly: indeed, I had written a book about them (which I had put away – it would be published sixteen years later) called *Make Believe*.

This disturbed my focus on large parts of *Guerrillas*. The people in the book were not meant to be portraits of those I had known (Vidia had met none of them). They were characters created by Vidia to express his view of post-colonial history in places like Trinidad. But the situation in the novel was so close to the situation in life that I often found it hard to repress the reaction 'But that's not true!'. This did not apply to the novel's Michael X character, who was called Jimmy Ahmed: Jimmy and the half-squalid half-pathetic ruins of his 'commune' are a brilliant and wholly convincing creation. Nor did it apply to Roche, Vidia's substitute for Hakim Jamal. Roche is a liberal white South African refugee working for a big commercial firm, whose job has involved giving cynical support to Jimmy. Roche was so evidently not Hakim that the question did not arise. But it certainly did apply to Jane, who stood in for Gail in being the murdered woman.

The novel's Jane, who comes to the island as Roche's mistress, is supposed to be an idle, arid creature who tries to find the vitality she lacks by having affairs with men. Obtuse in her innate sense of her superiority as a white woman, she drifts into such an attempt with Jimmy: an irresponsible fool playing a dangerous game for kicks with a ruined black man. Earlier, Vidia had written an account for a newspaper of Gail's murder which made it clear that he saw Gail as that kind of woman.

She was not. She was idle and empty, but she had no sense of her own superiority as a white woman or as anything else. Far from playing dangerous games for kicks, she was clinging on to illusions for dear life. The people she had most in common with were not the kind of secure Englishwomen who had it off with black men to demonstrate their own liberal attitudes, but those poor wretches who followed the American 'guru' Jones to Guyana in 1977, and ended by committing mass suicide at his bidding. She was so lacking in a sense of her own worth that it bordered on insanity.

It was therefore about Jane that I kept saying to myself 'But that's not true!'. Then I pulled myself together and saw that there was no reason why Jane should be like Gail: an Englishwoman going into such an affair for kicks was far from impossible and would be a perfectly fair example of fraudulence of motive in white liberals, which was what Vidia was bent on showing.

So I read the book again – and this time Jane simply fell to pieces. Roche came out of it badly, too: a dim character, hard to envisage, in spite of revealing wide-apart molars with black roots whenever he smiled (a touch of 'clever characterization' which should have been beneath Vidia). But although he doesn't quite convince, he almost does; you keep expecting him to emerge from the mist. While Jane becomes more and more like a series of bits and pieces that don't add up, so that finally her murder is without significance. I came to the conclusion that the trouble must lie with Vidia's having cut his cloth to fit a pattern he had laid down in advance: these characters existed in order to exemplify his argument, he had not been *discovering* them. So they did not live; and the woman lived less than the man because that is true of all Vidia's women.

We have now reached the second of my two shocking failures as an editor (I don't intend ever to confess the other one). From the professional point of view there was no question as to what I ought to do: this was one of our most valuable authors; even if his book had been really bad rather than just flawed we would certainly have published it in the expectation that he would soon be back on form; so what I must say was 'wonderful' and damn' well sound as though I meant it.

Instead I sat there muttering: 'Oh my God, what am I going to say to him?' I had never lied to him – I kept reminding myself of that, disregarding the fact that I had never before needed to lie. 'If I lie now, how will he be able to trust me in the future when I praise something?' The obvious answer to that was that if I lied convincingly he would never know that I had done it, but this did not occur to me. After what seemed to me like hours of sincere angst I ended by persuading myself that I 'owed it to our friendship' to tell him what I truly thought.

Nothing practical would be gained. A beginner writer sometimes makes mistakes which he can remedy if they are pointed out, but a novelist of Vidia's quality and experience who produces an unconvincing character has suffered a lapse of imagination about which nothing can be done. It happened to Dickens whenever he attempted a good woman; it happened to George Eliot with Daniel Deronda. And as for my own attitude – I had often seen through other people who insisted on telling the truth about a friend's shortcomings: I knew that *their* motives were usually suspect. But my own were as invisible to me as a cuttlefish becomes when it saturates the surrounding water with ink.

So I told him. I began by saying how much I admired the many things in the book which I did admire, and then I said that I had to tell him (*had to* tell him!) that two of his three central characters had failed to convince me. It was like saying to Conrad 'Lord Jim is a very fine novel except that Jim doesn't quite come off'.

Vidia looked disconcerted, then stood up and said quietly that he was sorry they didn't work for me, because he had done the best he could with them, there was nothing more he could do, so there was no point in discussing it. As he left the room I think I muttered something about its being a splendid book all the same, after which I felt a mixture of relief at his appearing to be sorry rather than angry, and a slight (only slight!) sense of let-down and silliness. And I supposed that was that.

The next day Vidia's agent called André to say that he had been instructed to retrieve *Guerrillas* because we had lost confidence in Vidia's writing and therefore he was leaving us.

André must have fought back because there was nothing he hated more than losing an author, but the battle didn't last long. Although I believe I was named, André was kind enough not to blame me. Nor did I blame myself. I went into a rage. I fulminated to myself, my colleagues, my friends: 'All those years of friendship, and a mere dozen words of criticism – *a mere dozen words!* – send him flouncing out in a tantrum like some hysterical prima donna!' I had long and scathing conversations with him in my head; but more satisfying was a daydream of being at a huge and important party, seeing him enter the room, turning on my heel and walking out.

For at least two weeks I seethed . . . and then, in the third week, it suddenly occurred to me that never again would I have to listen to Vidia telling me how damaged he was, and it was as though the sun came out. *I didn't have to like Vidia any more!* I could still like his work, I could still be sorry for his pain; but I no longer faced the task of fashioning affection out of these elements in order to deal as a good editor should with the exhausting, and finally tedious, task of listening to his woe. 'Do you know what,' I said to André, 'I've begun to see that it's a release.' (Rather to my surprise, he laughed.) I still, however, failed to see that my editorial 'mistake' had been an act of aggression. In fact I went on failing to see that for years.

Guerrillas was sold to Secker & Warburg the day after it left us.

A month or so after this I went into André's office to discuss something and his phone rang before I had opened my mouth. This always happened. Usually I threw myself back in my chair with a groan, then reached for something to read, but this time I jumped up and grabbed the extension. 'Why – Vidia!' he had said. 'What can I do for you?'

Vidia was speaking from Trinidad, his voice tense: André must call his agent *at once* and tell him to recover the manuscript of *Guerrillas* from Secker & Warburg and deliver it to us.

André, who was uncommonly good at rising to unexpected occasions, became instantly fatherly. Naturally, he said, he would be

delighted to get the book back, but Vidia must not act too impetu-
ously: whatever had gone wrong might well turn out to be less
serious that he now felt. This was Thursday. What Vidia must do
was think it over very carefully without taking action until Monday.
Then, if he still wanted to come back to us, he must call his agent,
not André, listen to his advice, and if that failed to change his mind,
instruct him to act. André would be waiting for the agent's call on
Monday afternoon or Tuesday morning, hoping – of course – that
it would be good news for us.

Which – of course – it was. My private sun did go back behind
a film of cloud, but in spite of that there was satisfaction in knowing that he thought himself better off with us than with them, and
I had no doubt of the value of whatever books were still to come.

Vidia never said why he bolted from Secker's, but his agent told
André that it was because when they announced *Guerrillas* in their
catalogue they described him as 'the West Indian novelist'.

The books still to come were, indeed, worth having (though the last
of them was his least important): *India, a Wounded Civilization*,
The Return of Eva Peron, *Among the Believers*, *A Bend in the River*
and *Finding the Centre*. I had decided that the only thing to do was
to behave exactly as I had always done in our pre-*Guerrillas* working relationship, while quietly cutting down our extra-curricular
friendship, and he apparently felt the same. The result was a
smooth passage, less involving but less testing than it used to be.
Nobody else knew – and I myself was unaware of it until I came to
look back – that having resolved never again to utter a word of
criticism to Vidia, I was guilty of an absurd pettiness. In *Among the
Believers*, a book which I admired very much, there were two minor
points to which in the past I would have drawn his attention, and

I refrained from doing so: thus betraying, though luckily only to my retrospecting self, that I was still hanging on to my self-righteous interpretation of the *Guerrillas* incident. Vidia would certainly not have 'flounced out like some hysterical prima donna' over matters so trivial. One was a place where he seemed to draw too sweeping a conclusion from too slight an event and could probably have avoided giving that impression by some quite small adjustment; and the other was that when an Iranian speaking English said 'sheep' Vidia, misled by his accent, thought he said 'ship', which made some dialogue as he reported it sound puzzling. To keep mum about that! There is nothing like self-deception for making one ridiculous.

When Vidia really did leave us in 1984 I could see why – and even why he did so in a way which seemed unkind, without a word of warning or explanation. He had come to the conclusion that André Deutsch Limited was going downhill. It was true. The recession, combined with a gradual but relentless shrinkage in the readership of books such as those we published, was well on the way to making firms of our size and kind unviable; and André had lost his vigour and flair. His decision to sell the firm, which more or less coincided with Vidia's departure, was made (so he felt and told me) because publishing was 'no fun any more', but it was equally a matter of his own slowly failing health. The firm continued for ten years or so under Tom Rosenthal, chuntering not-so-slowly downwards all the time (Tom had been running Secker's when they called Vidia a West Indian, so his appearance on the scene did nothing to change Vidia's mind).

A writer of reputation can always win an even bigger advance than he is worth by allowing himself to be tempted away from publisher A by publisher B, and publisher B will then have to try extra hard on his behalf to justify the advance: it makes sense to move on if you time it right. And if you perceive that there is something going seriously wrong with publisher A you would be foolish not to do so. And having decided to go, how could you look in the eye someone you have known for over twenty years, of whom you have been really quite fond, and tell him 'I'm leaving because you are getting past it'? Of course you could not. Vidia's agent managed to conceal from André what Vidia felt, but André suspected something: he told me that he thought it was something to do with himself and that he couldn't get it out of the agent, but perhaps I might have better luck. I called the agent and asked him if there was any point in my getting in touch with Vidia, and he – in considerable embarrassment – told me the truth; whereupon I could only silently agree with Vidia's silence, and tell poor André that I'd been so convincingly assured of the uselessness of any further attempt to change Vidia's mind that we had better give up.

So this leaving did not make me angry, or surprised, or even sad, except for André's sake. Vidia was doing what he had to do, and it seemed reasonable to suppose that we had enjoyed the best of him, anyway. And when many years later Mordecai Richler (in at the story's end, oddly enough, as well as its beginning) told me that he had recently met Vidia with his new wife and had been pleased to see that he was 'amazingly jolly', I was very glad indeed.

MOLLY KEANE

I KNOW THAT I have sometimes been described as 'one of the best editors in London', and I can't deny that it has given me pleasure; but I also know how little I had to do to earn this reputation beyond routine work and being agreeable to interesting people. And another example of this is my dealings with the person I liked best among those I came to know on the job: the Irish novelist Molly Keane.

It is common knowledge that after establishing herself in her youth as a novelist and playwright, Molly went silent for over thirty years and was 'rediscovered' in 1981 when André Deutsch Limited published *Good Behaviour*. Because I was her editor I was often congratulated on this 'rediscovery' – which is nonsense. We got the book by pure luck.

The person who persuaded Molly to offer it for publication was Peggy Ashcroft, who had remained a close friend of hers since acting in one of her plays, and who said one day, when staying with her, how sad it was that she had stopped writing. Molly told

her that she had recently started again and had a novel which she
was unsure about tucked away in a drawer. Peggy insisted on taking
it to bed with her that night, and as a result of her enthusiasm
Molly sent it to Ian Parsons of Chatto & Windus. That was where
our good luck began: Ian didn't like it. Worse mistakes have been
made – publishers often used to console themselves by remembering that André Gide, reading Proust's *Remembrance of Things Past*,
turned it down ... although if you envisage that enormous manuscript, and discovering that many of its sentences are as long as
most people's paragraphs, that mistake was perhaps less *odd* than
failing to respond to a novel as accessible as *Good Behaviour*.

Our next stroke of luck was that Molly then chose Gina Pollinger
as her agent. Gina had been an editor before she married into
agenting, and her last job as such had been with us. When she
called me to say that she had just read something she loved, and felt
sure I would love it too, I was hearing from someone whose taste I
knew and respected, rather than listening to a sales spiel, so naturally I read the book at once – and it happened that I, unlike Ian
Parsons, had not fallen on my head. So much for being Molly's
rediscoverer.

Molly did usually need a little editing because she could get into
muddles about timing – make, for instance, an event happen after
an interval of two years when something in the text revealed that at
least three years must have passed – and she had little tricks of
phrasing, such as describing a person's interests as her 'importances',
which she sometimes overdid. (Such tricks are part of a writer's
'voice', so it is usually best to leave some of them in – but not enough
of them to be annoying.) She was always glad to have such things
pointed out, and she was equally co-operative over the only big
question that needed solving in the course of her last three novels.

This occurred in *Good Behaviour*, at a point where a small English boy is discovered hiding up a tree in order to read poetry, which causes his extremely upper-class parents to go into paroxysms of dismay. At that point Molly's sense of comedy had taken the bit between its teeth and bolted, carrying the story off into the realm of the grotesque. It was wildly funny, but funny in a way at odds with the rest of the book so that it fractured its surface. I asked her to cool it, which she did. She was always 'splendidly cooperative to work with', as John Gielgud was to say in a letter to the *Daily Telegraph* after her death, remembering the days when he directed the four plays which she wrote in the thirties.

He also paid a warm tribute to her charm and wit, adding that 'she was endlessly painstaking and industrious' – slightly surprising words applied to someone as sparkly as Molly, but they do catch the absence of pretentiousness in her attitude to her work. Her background was that of the Irish landed gentry, whose daughters were lucky, in her day, if they got more than a scrappy education. Not that most of them, including Molly, were likely to clamour for more, since horses and men interested them far more than anything else; but Molly had come to feel the lack and it made her humble: she needed to be convinced that she was a good writer.

She was well aware, however, that *Good Behaviour* was different from the eleven early novels which she had written under the pen-name M. J. Farrell – a pen-name because who would want to dance with a girl so brainy that she wrote books? (You probably need to have had a 'county' upbringing fully to feel the withering effect of that adjective: 'You're the brainy one, aren't you?' It still makes me flinch.) Molly always said that she wrote the early books simply for money, because her parents couldn't afford to give her a dress allowance – though the verve of the writing suggests that she must have enjoyed doing it. *Good Behaviour*, on the other hand, had insisted on being written. She described it as a book that 'truly interested and involved' her: 'Black comedy, perhaps, but with some of the truth in it, and the pity I feel for the kind of people I lived with and laughed with in the happy maligned thirties.' She said that she dropped the pen-name because so much time had gone by; but in fact she took a lot of urging, and left me with the impression that she finally agreed because she had allowed herself to be persuaded that this one was the real thing.

The reason why *Good Behaviour* is so gripping is that Molly brings off something much cleverer than she had ever attempted before: she manoeuvres her readers into collaboration. Her narrator, Aroon St Charles, the large, clumsy daughter of a remote and elegant little mother who finds her painfully boring, tells us everything she sees – and often fails to understand what she is telling. It is up to us, the readers, to do the understanding – most crucially concerning Aroon's beloved brother Hubert and the friend he brings home from Cambridge, Richard Massingham (once the little boy who read poetry up a tree). Aroon has never heard of homosexuality, because the rules of Good Behaviour are the rules of behaving 'as if'. You may be afraid but you must behave as if you were brave; you may be poor but you must behave as if you can afford things; your husband may be randy but you must behave as if he wasn't; embarrassing things such as men falling in love with men may happen, but you must behave as if they don't. How could Aroon, who doesn't read and has few friends, know anything about being gay? But in spite of all the 'as iffing', her father starts to feel uneasy about the two young men, they become alarmed – and Hubert has a brilliant idea: Richard must start behaving as though he were courting Aroon. He must even go into her bedroom one night, and make sure that her father hears him leaving it . . . We hear nothing of all this but what Aroon tells us: that Richard does this, and Richard does that, so surely he must like her – must even be finding her attractive – must *love* her! After he has been to her room we see her half-sensing that something is wrong (his Respecting her Virginity is acceptable, but there is something about his manner . . .). And we see her, very soon, working herself into a blissful daze of happiness at having a lover. And all the time, as though we were observant guests in the house, *we can see what is really going on*. It is powerfully involving, and it continues through-out the book: at one point thirty pages go by before we are allowed a flash of understanding (the family lawyer has made a tentative pass at Aroon, which seems a bit odd – until the times comes, as it would do in 'real life', when one exclaims 'But of course! He knew what was in her father's will!').

Molly called this book 'black comedy', and comic it often is – brilliantly so. She is studying tribal behaviour, and no one could hit off its absurdities to better effect. But its strength comes from her fierce, sad knowledge of what underlies Good Behaviour, and is crippled by it; and she once told me something about herself which struck me as the seed from which this novel's power grew.

Molly's husband Robert Keane died in his thirties, with appalling suddenness, when they were visiting London with their two little daughters, having a very good time. He became violently ill so that he had to be rushed to hospital, but once he was there everything seemed to be under control, so she went back to the children for the night, worried but not really frightened. During the night the tele-phone rang. It was the hospital matron, who said: 'Mrs Keane, you must be brave. Your husband is dead.' Molly had friends in London, but they were busy theatre friends, and she was seized at once by the thought 'I must not be a nuisance. I must not make scenes' – the quintessential Good Behaviour reaction. And some time during those terrible first days her eldest daughter, Sally, who was six, clutched her hand and said: 'Mummy, we mustn't cry, we mustn't cry.'

And Molly never did cry. Forty years later, telling me that, her voice took on a tone of forlorn incredulity. There was, indeed, nothing she didn't know about her tribe's concept of good behaviour, in all its gallantry, absurdity and cruelty.

The part of the novel which calls most directly on her personal experience of clamping down on pain is so quietly handled that I believe it sometimes escapes quick readers. On their way back to Cambridge in Richard's car the boys are involved in a crash and Hubert is killed. It is easy to see that when the news comes his stricken parents behave impeccably according to their lights: no scenes, not a tear – the deep chill of sorrow evident only in the rigidity of their adherence to the forms of normality. But there comes a day when Aroon can't resist pretending to her father that Richard truly was her lover and he says 'Well, thank God' which puzzles her a little; but his leaving her rather suddenly to visit the young horses down on the bog (so he says) ends their talk. And on that same day her mother has gone out, carrying a little bunch of cyclamen, and Aroon has wondered where she is off to. And it never occurs to her that both parents are slipping off to visit Hubert's grave in secret; that only guiltily can they allow their broken hearts this indulgence. That her father is felled by a stroke in the graveyard, not the bog, and that her mother, who comes screaming back to the house in search of help, was there with him . . . in the commotion and horror of it all Aroon makes no comment on this, and again it is left to the reader to understand.

*

It is impossible for someone of great natural charm to remain unaware of the effect he or she has on others, which makes the gift a dangerous one: the ability to get away with murder demands to be exploited, and over-exploited charm can be less attractive than charmlessness. Molly Keane was remarkable in being both one of the most charming people I ever met, and an entirely successful escaper from that attendant danger.

Of course she knew how winning she could be. She once said to me: 'When I was young I'm afraid I used to sing for my supper,' meaning that when she first met people more interesting and sophisticated than her own family she won herself a warm welcome, in spite of being neither pretty nor well-dressed, by her funniness and charm. She needed to do this because she was too intelligent for her background and her mother had made her feel an ugly duckling, and a delinquent one at that (probably, like many unloved children, she did respond by being tiresome from her parents' point of view). Being taken up by people who were charmed by her was her salvation, and winning them over did not end by making her unspontaneous or manipulative because her clear sight, sensitivity, honesty and generosity were even stronger than her charm. By the time I knew her, when she was in her seventies, she would occasionally resort to 'turning it on' in order to get through an interview or some fatiguing public occasion, and very skilfully she did it; but otherwise she was always more interested in what was happening around her, and in the people she was meeting, than she was in the impression she was making, so even on a slight acquaintance it was the woman herself one saw, not a mask, and the woman was lovable.

In spite of liking her so much I have to consider my acquaintance with her as less than a friendship, properly speaking. Someone in her seventies with two daughters to love, a wide circle of acquaintances and an unusually large number of true and intimate friends of long standing, hasn't much room in her life for new close friends. I see that only too clearly now that I have overtaken the age Molly had reached when we met: one feels almost regretful on recognizing exceptionally congenial qualities in a newly met person, because one knows one no longer has the energy to clear an adequate space for them. When Molly and I exchanged letters about her work I was always tempted by her image in my mind to run on into gossip and jokes, while hers were quick scrawls about the matter under discussion; and enjoyable though our meetings were when she came to London, they didn't much advance the intimacy between us, and I sometimes thought I discerned in them a courteously disguised distaste for an important aspect of my life: the fact that I live with a black man. Molly was well aware of how others could see attitudes belonging to her background and gener-ation, such as disliking left-wing politics and mixed marriages; but an attitude is not necessarily *quite* expunged by knowing that it is not respectable.

Only once did I spend more than a meal-time with her. We gave a launching party for *Good Behaviour* in Dublin, I decided to take my car over and stay on for a ten-day holiday, and Molly invited me to stay with her for (I thought) the weekend at the start of the hol-iday. After the party I drove her to her home in Ardmore, and learnt on the way that she had arranged parties for me on every day of the coming week and had told a friend that she was bringing me to stay with him for two nights at the end of it. At first I was slightly dismayed by this unexpected abundance of hospitality, but I was soon enjoying every minute of it.

Partly this was because of the difference between Counties

Cork and Waterford and my native East Anglia. Most of the people we met were the Irish equivalent of my family's friends: country gentlefolk preoccupied with hunting, shooting, farming, gardening . . . the very people I had escaped from (so I had felt, fond though I was of many of them) when I moved on from Oxford to earn my living in London. Had I been faced with a week of parties given by Norfolk people of that kind who were strangers to me I would have seen it as a grim ordeal by boredom – and it *would* have been pretty boring because my hosts, given the tedious duty of entertaining a foreign body, and I as the reluctant victim of their hospitality, would between us have erected an impenetrable wall of polite small-talk from which eventually both sides would have retreated in a state of exhaustion. But in Ireland . . . much as I distrust generalizations about national characteristics, there's no denying that most Irish people are more articulate than the English, appearing to see talk as a positive pleasure rather than a tiresome necessity. I don't suppose I shared many more interests with my Irish hosts than I would have done with English ones (although I did know quite a lot about theirs) – but they were so much more lively and witty, and so much readier to start or to follow a new trail, than the people among whom I was raised, that whether or not interests were shared didn't seem to matter. All the parties were thoroughly enjoyable.

They were given an appetizing touch of spice by the stories Molly told on the way to them about the people we were going to meet, which were splendidly indiscreet. If she disliked someone she either kept silent or spoke briefly with indignant disapproval; with the rest she rejoiced in their follies, if follies they displayed, but as a fascinated observer rather than a censorious judge. Perhaps

novelists are so often good at gossip because – like God with forgiveness – *c'est leur métier*.

On one of those drives she gave me a gleeful glimpse of local
standards of literary criticism. An elderly neighbour, blue-blooded
but rustic in her ways (I gathered that she usually kept her gum-
boots on and her false teeth out) had said to her: 'I read your book,
Molly, and I absolutely *hated* it – but I must say that it was very well
written. I didn't find a single spelling mistake.'

The drives, and the time spent alone with Molly in her house
tucked into the hillside overlooking Ardmore and its bay, were even
better than the parties. She was an exquisitely kind and considerate
hostess, but it wasn't that which made the visit so memorable. It
was the extent to which Molly was alive to everything around her –
to the daughters she worried about and adored, the people she
knew, the events she remembered, her garden, the food she cooked,
the problems and satisfactions of writing. And it was also the fact
that day by day I became more aware of the qualities she kept
hidden: her courage, her unselfishness – simply her goodness.

The chief difference, it seems to me, between the person who is
lucky enough to possess the ability to create – whether with words
or sound or pigment or wood or whatever – and those who haven't
got it, is that the former react to experience directly and each in his
own way, while the latter are less ready to trust their own responses
and often prefer to make use of those generally agreed to be acceptable by their friends and relations. And while the former certainly
include by far the greater proportion of individuals who would be
difficult to live with, they also include a similarly large proportion
of individuals who are exciting or disturbing or amusing or inspiring to know. And Molly, in addition to having charm and being
good, was also a creator.

I am glad, therefore, that our last exchange of letters was about her writing, and not just one of general well-wishing (as they had been for some years, since she became seriously ill with heart trouble). I had just reread *Good Behaviour* for some forgotten reason, and on meeting Molly's daughter Virginia as we walked our dogs, had told her how greatly I had re-enjoyed it. Virginia urged me to write and tell Molly, saying that although the worst of her depression at being weak and helpless had lifted, she still needed cheering up. So I wrote her a long letter about why I love that book so much, and also her last book, *Loving and Giving*, and said that although I knew she was downcast at not having been able to write another book, she surely must acknowledge that what she had done had been marvellously well done – that her writing had, in fact, won laurels on which anyone should be proud to rest. She replied that my letter had done her good and had lifted her depression about her writing 'right off the ground', then went on to say very sweetly how much she valued my opinion, ending with words which I knew to be valedictory, of such generosity that I can only treasure them.

I feel a real loss at losing your company. I shan't get to London again and I'm too weak and foolish to ask you to come here. But we have had many good moments together and you have done *everything* for my books – *think* what that has meant to me, to my life. With my love and thanks. Molly

By 'doing everything' for her books she meant that if we had not published *Good Behaviour*, *Time After Time* and *Loving and Giving*, her earlier books would not have been reissued in paperback by

Virago. The real originator of this sequence (not counting Ian
Parsons) was Gina Pollinger, as I am sure Molly recognized and
must have acknowledged with a similar generosity and more
reason; but I do still get great satisfaction from remembering that
Molly's reappearance under our imprint brought her serious recognition as a writer, and also put an end to the money problems that
had harassed her throughout her long widowhood. I do think of it,
as she bade me, and it makes me happy. Remembering that outcome, and the pleasure of knowing her, is a good way to end this
book.

POSTSCRIPT

Having seen André Deutsch Limited fade out, why am I not sadder than I am?

I suppose it is because, although I have often shaken my head over symptoms of change in British publishing such as lower standards of copy-preparation and proof-reading, I cannot feel that they are crucial. It is, of course, true that reading is going the same way as eating, the greatest demand being for the quick and easy, and for the simple, instantly recognizable flavours such as sugar and vinegar, or their mental equivalents; but that is not the terminal tragedy which it sometimes seems to the disgruntled old. It is not, after all, a new development: quick and easy has always been what the majority wants. The difference between my early days in publishing and the present is not that this common desire has come into being, but that it is now catered for more lavishly than it used to be. And that is probably because the grip on our trade of a particular caste has begun to relax.

Of that caste I am a member: one of the mostly London-

dwelling, university-educated, upper-middle-class English people
who took over publishing towards the end of the nineteenth century from the booksellers who used to run it. Most of us loved
books and genuinely tried to understand the differences between
good and bad writing; but I suspect that if we were examined from
a god's-eye viewpoint it would be seen that quite often our 'good'
was good only according to the notions of the caste. Straining for
that god's-eye view, I sometimes think that not a few of the books
I once took pleasure in publishing were pretty futile, and that the
same was true of other houses. Two quintessentially 'caste' writers,
one from the less pretentious end of the scale, the other from its
highest reaches, were Angela Thirkell and Virginia Woolf. Thirkell
is embarrassing – I always knew that, but would have published her,
given the chance, because she was so obviously a seller. And Woolf,
whom I revered in my youth, now seems almost more embarrassing because the claims made for her were so high. Not only did she
belong to the caste, but she was unable to see beyond its bound-
aries – and that self-consciously 'beautiful' writing, all those
adjectives – oh dear! Caste standards – it ought not to need saying –
have no right to be considered sacrosanct.

Keeping that in mind is a useful specific against melancholy;
and even better is the fact that there are plenty of people about who
are making a stand against *too much* quick-and-easy. The speed
with which the corners of supermarkets devoted to organic produce are growing into long shelves is remarkable; and there are still
publishers – not many, but some – who are more single-mindedly
determined to support serious writing than we ever were.

I have just visited one: the first time in seven years that I have set
foot in a publisher's office. It astonished me: how familiar it was,
the way I knew what was happening behind its doors . . . and how

much I loved it. 'It's still there!' I said to myself; and on the way home I saw that by 'it' I meant not only publishing of a kind I recognized, but something even more reassuring: being young. Old people don't want to mop and mow, but age has a blinkering effect, and their narrowed field of vision often contains things that *are* going from bad to worse; it is therefore consoling to be reminded that much exists outside that narrow field, just as it did when we were forty or thirty or twenty.

Finding myself not gravely distressed by the way publishing is changing seems reasonable enough. I am harder put to understand how anyone can feel in their bones, as I can, that life is worth living when every day we see such alarming evidence that a lot of it is unacceptable: that idiocy and cruelty, far from being brought to heel by human ingenuity, are as rampant as ever. I suppose the answer lies in something of which that small publishing house is a part.

Years ago, in a pub near Baker Street, I heard a man say that humankind is seventy per cent brutish, thirty per cent intelligent, and though the thirty per cent is never going to win, it will always be able to leaven the mass just enough to keep us going. That rough and ready assessment of our plight has stayed with me as though it were true, given that one takes 'intelligence' to mean not just intellectual agility, but whatever it is in beings that makes for readiness to understand, to look for the essence in other beings and things and events, to respect that essence, to collaborate, to discover, to endure when endurance is necessary, to enjoy: briefly, to co-exist. It does, alas, seem likely that sooner or later, either through our own folly or a collision with some wandering heavenly body, we will all vanish in the wake of the dinosaurs; but until that happens I believe that the yeast of intelligence will continue to operate one way or another.

Even if it operates in vain, it remains evolution's peak (as far as we can see): something to enjoy and foster as much as possible; something not to betray by succumbing to despair, however deep the many pits of darkness. It even seems to me possible dimly to perceive it as belonging not to a particular planet, but to universal laws of being, potentially present anywhere in the universe where the kind of physical (or should it be chemical?) conditions prevail which kindle life out of dust: an aspect of something which human beings have called by the various names of god, because having no name for it made them feel dizzy.

In the microscopic terms of my own existence, believing this means that in spite of reading the newspapers, and in spite of seeing the sad end of André's brave endeavour, and in spite of losing a considerable part of my youth to heartbreak, I wake up every morning *liking* being here. (I apologize to André, and to my young self, for being able to dismiss so lightly events which were once so painfully heavy.) I also wake up knowing that I have been extraordinarily lucky, and a good chunk of that luck came with the job. When I was moved to scribble 'Stet' against the time I spent being an editor it was because it gave so many kinds of enlargement, interest, amusement and pleasure to my days. It was a job on the side of the thirty per cent.